The Habit Guide

The Habit Guide

Zen Habits'
Effective Habit Methods + Solutions

Leo Babauta

WAKING LION PRESS

ISBN 978-1-4341-0473-1

Cover design by Spyr.

Published by Waking Lion Press, an imprint of the Editorium, LLC.

Waking Lion Press™ and Editorium™ are trademarks of:

The Editorium, LLC
West Jordan, UT 84081-6132
www.editorium.com

Contents

Introduction: Why Habits Are Important

When I was struggling with lots of areas in my life, I couldn't figure out what was wrong with me.

Why couldn't I stick to any of the exercise plans I'd chosen from magazines? Why couldn't I eat healthier, quit smoking, get my finances in order? Why couldn't I stop procrastinating, finally write that book I'd always planned to write.

Why couldn't I get anything going?

The answer, it turns out, was pretty simple: I had bad habits, and I didn't know how to change them.

I approached a new project, a new exercise or eating plan in the same way that most people approach it: I simply said I would do it.

Going to exercise regularly? All I had to do was put "exercise" on my calendar or to-do list, or just remember to do it, right?

Of course, when it came time to actually doing it, I was busy with a million daily things I had to do for work or my personal life. Or I just didn't feel like it, so I didn't do it.

Then I figured out how habits work.

I researched habits, so that I could figure out how to finally quit smoking (I'd tried and failed to quit seven times already). I read articles, research papers, advice from the

American Cancer Society, and more. I put a hundred techniques into action, and some of them worked!

I used the same ideas to start running, eating healthier, decluttering, becoming more focused and productive, and generally starting to change dozens of habits.

My life changed completely.

I learned that habits are extremely important in changing your life. Here's why.

1. If you want to reach a goal, you could just say, "I'm going to work towards this goal regularly." And hope for the best. Or you could form a habit that gets you to that goal—run daily if you want to finish a marathon, for example, or practice daily if you want to learn guitar.

2. If you put a lot of focus and effort into creating a new habit for a month, it will become fairly automatic, so you don't need to focus on it as much. After a month, you could work on a second habit, and so on, and after a year of doing this you could have 10–12 new habits. Instead, you could try focusing on 10–12 projects or life changes at once—it's a juggling act that's not very sustainable. Creating habits one at a time is much more sustainable.

3. Through habit experimentation, you learn your obstacles and learn what environment works best for you. For example, if you are trying to learn to beat procrastination, you learn that you have obstacles when it comes to facing scary tasks, when it comes to running towards distraction, when it comes to rationalizing those distractions. And you can find a system that helps you to overcome those obstacles, like accountability, mindfulness practices, and an Internet distraction blocker

These three reasons are pretty big. But the biggest reason to focus on changing habits is this: **by learning how to stick to small changes, you learn to trust yourself.** That's huge.

What I'm suggesting is that you learn, over the course of this book, to stick to one small change. That's it. Just a tiny change that's so easy you can't say no. One small change that will prove to yourself that you're trustworthy, that you can actually accomplish change.

And with that, you'll unlock the door to many other small changes. Over the course of months, that adds up to huge, sweeping change that can be unlike anything you've ever experienced.

Part I

HOW TO STICK TO A HABIT

In this main section of the book, I show how a habit is formed, why we have trouble sticking to new habits, and my most effective techniques for overcoming that obstacle.

This is the heart of the book, and if you take the time to practice some of these techniques, you'll get much better at sticking to habits. I highly encourage the practice.

Chapter 1

Overview of Habit Mechanics

The basics of creating a habit are pretty simple. But it's made complicated by the obstacles that get in the way.

We'll get to the obstacles soon, and some solutions for overcoming them. But first, let's do a quick overview of the basics.

The mechanics of creating a new habit work like this:

1. You pick a (preferably small) habit to stick to every day.

2. You pick a trigger to tie it to—something you already do every day, like eat breakfast or wake up in the morning.

3. You set up some kind of reminder so you don't forget to do the habit after the trigger.

4. You do the habit right after the trigger happens every day.

5. Ideally, positive feedback for doing the habit, and negative feedback for not doing the habit, will reinforce the continued doing of the habit.

6. After repeating this for awhile (let's say, 4–6 weeks), it becomes more and more automatic until you don't need reminders.

At this point, it's a pretty automatic habit. When the trigger happens, you'll automatically have the urge to do the habit.

Automaticity

How long you have to repeat this trigger-habit sequence before it becomes fairly automatic depends on a few things:

- How consistent you are with the habit (vs. how many days you miss).

- How easy the habit is (drinking a glass of water is easy, working out for 30 minutes is hard).

- How soon after the trigger you do the habit (should be immediately).

- How rewarding you find the habit (positive feedback). If the habit is a struggle, it's harder to become automatic.

It should be noted that habits aren't like flipping a switch— it's not like they become automatic after a certain number of repetitions. It's more like a spectrum, where they become more and more automatic over time. After a month, it's starting to be automatic, and after a few months it should be fairly automatic. If you do a habit consistently for years, it's very automatic.

If only creating habits were as simple as this! For some very easy habits, it's nearly as simple as the above steps. But for most habits you'll want to form, there are things that get in the way. That's what the rest of this book is designed to overcome.

Other Types Of Habits

Also note that this method is for habits that you do once a day, which I've found to be the easiest to form. There are other kinds of habits that you do with different frequencies:

1. Multiple times a day

2. Not every day but weekly or twice weekly

3. Only on weekdays or weekends

4. Irregularly and unpredictably (like when you go out with friends once in awhile, or get mad when someone irritates you)

These are harder to form. The multiple-times-a-day habits are harder to remember doing all day and you might not have the energy to keep it up for very many days. With the less-frequent habits, it often takes forever to do the habit enough times for it to become automatic, or you forget to do them. We'll go into these in a later chapter.

Another more advanced habit skill is **quitting bad habits**. These are habits you don't want, but have been doing them for so long that it's hard to break the trigger-habit bond. We'll get to those in another later chapter, but for now you should just know that these aren't good habits to start with.

Start with the easy stuff—new, positive habits that you're going to do once a day.

Chapter 2

Why People Struggle

If forming a habit is as simple as doing a small habit after a trigger every day . . . why isn't it an easier thing to do?

Because obstacles get in the way.

Things stop us from simply doing the habit after the trigger, so that we don't repeat the habit enough times for it to become automatic.

Some of the things that get in the way:

- **Resistance/procrastination**: We put off doing the habit, skipping it sometimes, because we don't feel like it, it's uncomfortable, it's easier to stick to our latest distractions. This is probably the biggest obstacle.

- **Busyness**: We have too much to do today, so we rush off to do all of it (a form of procrastination). Or a huge work project has caused us to be overwhelmed, a family crisis has taken all of our time, or we're traveling and can't do the habit. This actually does not need to be a huge problem, but missing the habit then causes us to have resistance to starting again.

- **Stories in our heads**: We're telling ourselves stories about our lives, including our habits and everything we have to do, all the time. Sometimes the stories are useful: "I'm going to be great at this habit and it's going to change my life!" But lots of times the stories are obstacles: "I can't do this, I suck at habits, I have no discipline, I keep failing, what's wrong with me?" This causes us resistance and we procrastinate.

- **Ideals/fantasies**: When we start a new habit and we're feeling excited about it, we have an ideal or a fantasy about the habit. Perhaps we believe it's going to change our lives in a positive way, it's going to give us peace and calm, it's going to make us productive or fit and healthy. This is not a problem, and is natural . . . but what happens if the reality doesn't meet the ideal? Maybe the exercise habit is much harder than we thought, filled with uncertainty and fear. We get discouraged. We then have resistance and we procrastinate.

As you can see, the last three obstacles all result in the first obstacle—resistance and procrastination. That's because they're all really the same thing, but in different forms.

In the end, the real reason we struggle with habits is because we let the stories or ideals in our heads cause resistance for us. And then we procrastinate.

So how do we solve this problem of resistance? We'll look at that in the next chapter.

Chapter 3

Overcoming Resistance and Procrastination

So we've identified the top culprit that causes us to struggle with habits: **resistance, and the procrastination that results.**

We have ideals and fantasies about the habit that aren't met. We get busy or travel and miss a day or two of the habit. We have stories in our heads that get in the way. All of these cause resistance and then procrastination.

How do we overcome these struggles?

This book is about this very question. I've found a number of ways to overcome resistance. They're not a "one size fits all" solution, though, so you'll have to try them to see what works best for you.

Here are my top ways to overcome resistance—we'll get into each in more detail in the following chapters:

1. **One habit at a time.** Most people have lots of habits they want to change, but it's a mistake to try to do them all at once. Taking on too many habits is a good way to overwhelm yourself (which is a source of resis-

tance). Pick one small habit to start with, and give it your complete focus.

2. **Small steps.** Making the habit as small as possible to start out with is my all-time favorite way to overcome resistance. If you only have to meditate for 2 minutes (instead of say, 30) then the resistance drops greatly.

3. **Deeper motivation.** If you have a really strong reason for wanting to do the habit, you'll overcome resistance. Lower the resistance and increase the motivation.

4. **Fully commit.** Lots of people just get started with a habit without a full commitment. I recommend deepening your commitment so that you don't back out when resistance comes up.

5. **Accountability.** Similarly, if you are held accountable by others, you're more likely to keep doing the habit even when you face resistance.

6. **Facing the resistance with mindfulness.** This is a mindfulness method for working with resistance that we'll talk about in a later chapter.

7. **Just getting started.** In this method, we don't worry about doing the entire habit, we just focus on the moment of starting. For example, instead of thinking about the habit of running, you focus on the habit of getting your running shoes on and getting out the door.

8. **Don't rely on "feeling like it".** This is a trick I've learned that works wonders for resistance—instead of skipping the habit because I "don't feel like it" . . . I just do it because that's the plan. The idea is that our use of "feeling like it" as a reason to do something or not do something is flawed. Instead, we should make a plan beforehand and just do it.

9. **Don't miss two days in a row.** It's easy to miss a day of doing the habit for various reasons, but it's not the end of the world. Just start again the next day. However, if you miss a second day, you become much less likely to continue. And if you miss a third, it's pretty unlikely you'll start again (unless you use some of the ideas below). It helps to have a rule that you won't miss two days in a row, no matter what.

10. **Getting through the Dip.** I've found the second or third week of a new habit can be somewhat of a slump for many people. I call it the Dip. You often start a habit with some enthusiasm, but that energy can run out after a couple of weeks. It's a critical point for most people, and you have to find a way to get re-motivated and make it through the Dip.

11. **Journaling and reflecting.** One of the best tools for sticking with a habit is journaling every day, or at least finding another way of reflecting on how it's going. This is because if there's some resistance coming up, some obstacle getting in the way, if you journal or reflect on it, you're less likely to give in to it without thinking. You can see the resistance and find a potential solution. You can reflect on whether your solutions are working and adjust if needed.

12. **Restarting and re-motivating.** Everyone misses a day of doing their habit sometimes. I've never met a person who was perfect at doing every single habit they attempted to form. Instead, the successful habit creators aren't the ones who are perfect, but the ones who learn to restart when they slip up. The ones who learn to re-motivate themselves when they feel disappointed or hit a slump.

13. **Changing your identity.** You can change how you see yourself. If you see yourself as someone who is bad

at exercise, for example, this can get in the way of forming the exercise habit. So you can try changing your identity, to someone who loves exercise. More on this later, but it can be surprisingly effective.

14. **Being completely present.** If you allow yourself to be completely present with the habit as you do it, it can be a form of meditation. In this way, it can actually be a bit of a stress relief from our busy, chaotic days. Your new habit can be a rewarding activity if you focus on enjoying each minute of doing it. And you can mindfully see resistance and work with it as it arises.

This might seem like a lot of ideas to try out, but don't worry, you don't have to do them all. Nor do you have to do them all at once. Explore each one in turn, and see what works best for you.

Let's take a look at them one at a time in the chapters that follow.

Chapter 4

One Habit at a Time

I remember one of the breakthroughs for me when I first started successfully changing my habits, after years of habit failure, was deciding to focus on just one habit.

There were so many habits I wanted to change: get healthier and fitter, get out of debt, become more mindful, simplify my life, declutter, read more, write more, start a business, spend time with my kids.

And I wanted to do it all at once. So I tried to form multiple habits at once . . . because I thought I could, and I couldn't imagine putting any of them off for a few months. Unfortunately, this method didn't work for me, and I kept failing to create 5–10 habits at once. Go figure!

It was like a revelation when I decided I was going to pick just one habit at a time and focus completely on that habit.

I chose quitting smoking to start with, though now I wouldn't recommend quitting a bad habit as your first habit. Still, I was successful, because I put everything I had into that habit, *as if I were saving my own life*. Which I was.

Eventually, I ended up changing all of the habits on my list. One at time. Focusing on each habit completely, giving it everything I had, creating accountability and consequences and mindfulness around the habit.

I learned that each habit change is a full-on project in itself, and needs your full focus. I learned that I didn't have room in my life to do more than one habit at once. And I learned that changing one at a time is not only more effective, it leads to completely changing your life over the course of a year or two. It's amazing.

Pick a small but powerful habit to start with. I recommend one of these: two minutes of meditation or yoga, journaling for two minutes, doing a handful of pushups. Each of these is small but leads to lots of learning.

Chapter 5

Prioritizing Habits and Balancing Multiple Habits

Two of the biggest questions people have are:

1. I really want to change everything at once, but it's hard to balance multiple habits!

2. If I have to just pick one, how do I prioritize?

Let's address both of these questions.

Balancing Multiple Habits

As I said in the last chapter, I really really suggest doing one habit at a time. It's too hard to do multiple habits at once—it's possible, but you're just making things harder on yourself.

That said, eventually you'll finish the first habit and want to do a second. And then a third. And so you'll be balancing several habits at once. How do you manage that?

A few suggestions:

1. Don't start a second habit until the first feels pretty solid. It should be a lot easier and more automatic than when you first started. Don't be in a rush to start your second.

2. When you start your second habit, keep it super small. You still have the first habit going on, so be mindful of that and make things really easy on yourself by starting as tiny as possible.

3. Be slower and slower to add new habits after the second one. Let the previous habits become really solid, and get good at returning to them if you get disrupted, adding accountability and support from others if you need it.

4. Keep the previous habits small as you add new habits. If you're doing three habits at once, you're much more likely to succeed if you keep them all very small.

Yes, eventually you'll want to expand your habits beyond "tiny," but don't be in a rush.

Prioritizing Habits

Let's say you agree to do just one habit at a time. How do you choose which to start with when you have a couple dozen you want to form?

First, realize that you don't need to rush to form all habits at once. Yes, you'll want to form them all quickly, because you want to see all the great life changes right now! But realize this: you didn't form your current habits in one month—it took you years to form them. You're not going to change them all in one month either. It will take a year or two, possibly more.

So take a realistic long-term view of your habit changes. If you change one small habit per month, you'll have a dozen over the course of a year. That's great success! And you'll have two dozen over the course of two years.

Second, it doesn't matter which habits you start with . . . because you'll be changing a lot of habits over the course of the next two years. You're going to get to them all! So just pick an easy one and start with that, and then a second easy one and start with that. The most important things are that you're learning to be consistent, learning to get back on track when you get disrupted, learning to create an environment that will support your changes, and learning to trust yourself.

Third, see these habit changes as experiments. No, you don't know which habits will be best for you . . . but there's no way to know for sure until you find out through these experiments. So let go of having the "perfect" list of habits to work on, or the "perfect" order. Neither of these exist. Instead, just experiment and find out, and enjoy the learning experience!

Finally, I suggest picking habits that will help you form other habits. Some ideas:

- **Meditation** - I've found the mindfulness cultivated by a couple minutes of breath meditation each day helps you form other habits.

- **Journaling** - This habit encourages reflection, which is a powerful part of any habit experiment.

- **Walking** - A daily walk gets you active, starts you on the path to health, can be a social activity if you walk with others, or a reflective time if you walk alone.

- **Waking a bit earlier** - If you try to wake too early, it's difficult. But if you wake just 10 minutes earlier, you create time for your meditation or journaling habit. And once that becomes easier, you can wake 10 minutes earlier than that, and have a little time for another tiny habit. Do this process slowly!

- **Something easy** - Some people have tried putting their clothes in the hamper when they're done using them, or wiping the counter after eating. If you start with an easy habit, you're building trust in yourself, and the skills you need to be consistent.

These are just a few ideas—you might consider making a list of good habits you want to form (not bad habits you want to quit, yet), then seeing which would be easiest and also might support the other habits on the list.

Some Questions about Priorities

Some readers submitted questions I'd like to answer here:

Question: I'm feeling overwhelmed by the number of habits I want to incorporate into my routine.

Answer: Yes, it can feel overwhelming! But this is a good opportunity to practice dealing with this feeling. You're attached to wanting to do everything, but it's not possible to do that right now. All you can do is focus on one habit, and try to get that to stick. Enjoy that process, really learn about it, because it will help you with all future habits. Really commit to one habit, and make it work. Then you can worry about the next one, but for now, don't worry about all the habits you need to form. Just the one you can take on right now.

Question: I'm indecisive about which habit to commit to, so I end up doing nothing.

Answer: Yes, indecision can stop all of us! The key is to make a decision, accept that it won't be the "perfect" decision, and then really commit to it. Ask for help—make a short list of habits you want to start with, and ask a friend to help you choose. Or have them choose for you, and commit to completely focusing on whatever habit they choose. Or roll a die, and pick that way. Whatever method you choose, realize that it won't matter which one you start with—except I highly recommend not trying to quit a bad habit to start with. Choose a new good habit to form, and start small.

Chapter 6

Start Small, Take Tiny Steps

This is probably the most powerful technique in this entire book, and if you take away nothing else, I would recommend you learn this.

Pick one habit, and start as small as you can.

Then increase the habit only gradually, one tiny step at a time.

Why is this so important? **Because it overcomes resistance like nothing else.**

Think about it like this:

1. If you are busy and think you don't have time . . . you do have time if the habit just takes 2 minutes.

2. If the habit is uncomfortable, like exercise or meditation . . . it's not unbearably uncomfortable if it's just for two minutes.

3. If you have a million things to do today, you might be tempted to put off a bigger habit . . . but you're more likely to just do a quick, 2-minute habit.

It works like magic. If you're feeling resistance to doing the habit, make the habit smaller.

A good progression is to start with just two minutes, then if you're able to successfully stick to the habit for a week, add a minute in the second week. Then add another minute the third week, and so on. If that's too slow, feel free to add two minutes a week. **As long as it feels gradual and slower than you can handle.**

But only add time to your habit if you were consistent the previous week. If you're struggling, stay at the length you're at, or even drop it back from three minutes to two so that you can get more consistent.

Remember this rule: **it's always more important to do the habit consistently than it is to do it for longer**. That's because you're trying to form the trigger-habit bond by being consistent over time. You're running a marathon, not a sprint.

Chapter 7

Finding Time for Habits

A common habit problem is finding time and energy for creating new habits, when perhaps you're already working long hours. The good news is: you don't have to commit that much time.

Can you find 10 minutes a day? That's all you need to start with.

And yes, almost anyone can find 10 minutes a day. If you watch TV, watch videos online, check Facebook or other social media, read the news or blogs or other favorite websites, play video games . . . you can spare 10 minutes.

You could take 10 minutes you normally spend drinking coffee in the morning, and journal while you have coffee. You could take 10 minutes you normally read websites in the morning, and meditate. You could take 10 minutes at the end of the day, when you normally unwind by watching TV, and unwind by meditating or going for a short walk.

How can 10 minutes be enough? Well, if you just start with a 2-minute habit (like meditating or journaling for two minutes, or doing a few pushups), then you can easily fit it into a 10-minute block. You might need a minute to set up, and then another minute to log your habit or report to others. Altogether, it should take less than 10 minutes.

Eventually you'll want to do a 5-minute habit, maybe a 10-minute habit (though you shouldn't rush to expand your habit—take your time). In that case, you'll eventually need 15 minutes for the habit. But that's OK, you can slowly find the time by stealing a little here and there from other activities. Just 5 minutes is all you need to steal . . . you can do it!

I decided that waking a little earlier (just 10 minutes earlier) was important for finding the time for new habits. Again, it's not much, but it can make a huge difference in your life.

If you're already working long hours, don't rush to form a dozen new habits. Start with one small one, maybe add a second when that's pretty strong, but wait until you feel you can handle the load before adding a third. There's no reason to rush—take your time, and allow your life to slowly adjust to the new things you're adding.

In summary: start as small as possible, steal a little time from non-essential activities, don't be in a rush to add a bunch of new habits too quickly.

Questions: Overcommitting to Habits

A couple readers asked a question I'd like to answer here:

Question: I tend to bite off too much and overcommit to new habits, then give up as soon as it gets difficult.

Answer: Yes, this is a good thing to be aware of! Many of us overcommit to a new habit (or even multiple habits), because we're very optimistic and enthusiastic when we start out. However, it's so easy for life to get in the way and disruptions and big projects and crises to come up . . . and then we don't have all the time and energy for the habit that we initially had.

So again, start as small as possible, don't get carried away. Make the start as easy on yourself as possible, and you're much more likely to be consistent and stick with it. Which is the real goal here, not winning any ego points for doing a lot all at once.

Chapter 8

Remembering—Set Reminders for the Habit

One of the first reasons people often mess up the habit is they forget to do it in the first place. It's not automatic yet, so you need a reminder. After a few weeks, if you're fairly consistent, you probably won't need a reminder anymore, though it doesn't hurt to keep it for a few more weeks.

I actually recommend having more than one reminder—at least one digital reminder, and one physical one.

My favorite physical reminders include:

- A big note ("Meditate," for example) near where your trigger happens—for example, near your coffeemaker if starting your coffee in the morning is the trigger.

- A note on your laptop or phone, if that's the first thing you reach for in the morning.

- An object, like a little Buddha statue if you want to meditate, placed where you'll be sure to see it.

- The equipment you need for the habit—for example, running shoes or a meditation cushion—placed near your bed or somewhere else you'll be sure not to miss it.

- A rubber band or bracelet on your wrist, which is good if you are doing an irregular habit (like chewing your nails when you're nervous) and you don't know when the trigger will occur.

- A picture that reminds you why you're doing the habit—your kids, if you're doing it for their sake, for example.

Physical reminders, if placed where you'll see them when you're supposed to do the habit, are excellent.

Digital reminders are also very helpful. Some examples:

- A phone reminder or alarm.

- A calendar alert.

- A desktop picture/wallpaper on your computer that reminds you of the habit (or the reason you're doing the habit).

- An app (like a habit app or meditation app) that reminds you to do the habit.

- Your browser home page set to something related to the habit.

- An email reminder—automated, or from a good friend.

I suggest you pick one from the physical category and another from the digital category as you're getting started with your habit. A good combo to start with is a phone reminder and a note placed near your trigger. If that doesn't work for you, try another from each category, dropping the old ones if they weren't right for you. Eventually you'll find what works best.

Questions about Reminders

A couple good questions about reminders that people have asked:

Question: How can I set reminders that are unobtrusive to others?

Answer: My favorite reminders are physical—a small note somewhere you'll see it ("meditate" on a small piece of paper perhaps) or a small physical object like a rock or flower could serve as an unobtrusive reminder. Or put your running shoes, yoga mat, meditation cushion by your bed, perhaps. Another idea is to wear a bracelet or rubber band around your wrist as a way to remember.

But if you can't find physical reminder that's unobtrusive to others, try a digital reminder—maybe a phone reminder that goes off at the same time each day, an email reminder if you check email often, a desktop wallpaper or phone lock screen wallpaper that will remind you of your habit.

Question: My reminders tend to lose effectiveness over time—how can I combat this?

Answer: It's good that you're aware of this! You can combat it by noticing when your reminder isn't working, and setting up a physical reminder instead. Or ask others for help in reminding you. Create different digital reminders each week so you don't start ignoring them. Or make a huge commitment with a big consequence so you can't possibly ignore your reminders. The bigger the stakes, the less likely you are to forget.

Chapter 9

Deeper Motivation

Why do you want to form your habit? It's a question you should take a little time contemplating.

If the answer is something like, "It would be cool to journal every day," or "It would be nice to have abs," or something along those lines . . . then the reason isn't very strong. You aren't that motivated.

And the problem is that when you face resistance, **you aren't likely to push through that resistance if your motivation isn't very strong**. You're more likely to skip the habit on the days you feel resistance, feel guilty about it, and miss doing it the next day too.

If you have strong motivation, however, you're much more likely to push through the resistance. So what are some strong motivations?

Here are some examples (some will be stronger for some people than others):

- Your health is suffering and your doctor said you'll die if you don't change your diet.

- You badly need the money (from writing an ebook, for example) to feed your family.

- You are in physical pain and need to stretch, do yoga, and go walking to relieve the pain.

- You set up a really embarrassing consequence (you'll have to sing in front of a crowd, for example—if that's embarrassing for you) and you definitely aren't going to let that happen.

Those are pretty good motivations. But I've found that **the best motivations are emotional ones**. And the best emotional motivation, in my experience, is love.

For example, here are some deeper motivations that come from a place of love:

- You are doing this habit out of love for your family, to make a better life for them.

- You're trying to set a healthy example for your spouse or parents or siblings, in hopes of inspiring them to make healthy changes, out of love for them.

- You doing the habit with hopes of setting a good example for your kids, and perhaps inspiring them . . . out of love for them.

- You're doing this habit out of love for yourself, to make your life better, to make yourself healthier or happier.

- You want to create something that will help others, out of love for them.

In each of these examples, you are trying to help other people or yourself, out of love for them (or yourself). These are beautiful reasons, and if you think of your love for them, you might be moved emotionally. That's a great thing.

As you consider your habit, think about your Why. And have a deeper Why.

Then think of your deeper Why as you get started each day with the habit—let this emotional reason move you to push through the resistance.

Chapter 10

Fully Commit (and the Inertia of Starting)

When I first started trying to change my habits, I'd just get started. I'd say, "I'm going to write every morning, from now on," or "I'm going to quit smoking, starting today."

Guess how well that went? Starting a habit casually means you're not fully committed. It's like saying to someone, "Hey, why don't we get married today?" If you haven't given it a lot of thought, and you don't make a big commitment, you're not fully in it.

And then when the resistance comes up, you're out.

So fully commit to the habit. I suggest you make a big commitment, and even make a vow. A vow is something you hold sacred, and won't easily abandon when things get tough.

Here's how to make a big commitment and a vow:

1. **Give it some thought.** Ask yourself why you're doing this (as in the last chapter), why you're moved to commit to this. Ask how much time and effort this will take, and whether you have space for it. Ask whether you're all in or not.

2. **Write it down**. If you're not willing to write a few paragraphs about this habit, you're not fully committed. Write your commitment on paper, write a plan for reminders, accountability, and more. What will you do when resistance comes up?

3. **Make a vow**. Again, a vow is something you hold sacred. So make a vow, by yourself or in front of someone else. Write it down and then say it out loud: "I vow to meditate every day out of love for myself and my family."

4. **Make a big public commitment**. Tell everyone about it. Yes, sometimes telling people about your goal disperses your actual commitment to the goal, but you're going to take the next step (accountability) so it won't happen that way for you. Tell everyone on Facebook and Twitter and Instagram about your commitment to this new habit. Or email everyone you know. Tell everyone in your office. And ask everyone to ask you about it at least weekly.

5. **Ask people to hold you accountable**. A good friend will not let you off the hook for your commitment. Ask your best friends, your spouse, everyone you know you can count on, to hold you accountable. Ask them to check in with you, or promise to check in with them daily. Maybe even set an unmissable consequence (more on all this in upcoming chapters).

Compare the above process of making a big commitment with the idea of just slipping into the habit without a commitment. One will keep you on the path when resistance arises, the other probably won't.

The Inertia of Getting Started

When you're contemplating starting a new habit, there are two common scenarios:

1. You're super excited and you want to get started right away; or

2. You aren't super excited and you keep putting off getting started.

The second scenario, of procrastinating the start of a new habit because of inertia, is fixable.

Here's what I suggest:

1. **Ask someone for help**. Tell them you need a shove to get started, ask them to make you commit and check in with them, and then make a commitment and start.

2. **Make the habit super small**. This makes it easier to start—it should be so easy you can't say no.

3. **Figure out your deeper motivation** (as per the last chapter). This motivation should be stronger than the inertia. If it's not, consider finding another habit that's more important to you.

Chapter 11

Don't Overdo Your Habit

This will sound contradictory, coming directly after the chapter that asks you to "fully commit," but it's possible to overdo it in the beginning.

We often start very motivated, and set big goals like, "I will quit my Bad Habit cold turkey from now on" or "I will exercise for 30 minutes every day" . . . but then everything falls apart once we mess up a bit. If you fail to quit the Bad Habit, you feel guilty and feel like a failure. If you can't find the energy to exercise 30 minutes every single day, the entire habit can collapse.

How do we overcome this problem? **By starting small—** as I said, this is possibly the most important technique in creating a new habit.

First, don't start by trying to quit a bad habit. Lots of people have bad habits they want to quit, but you shouldn't even attempt it until you've formed several good habits first (like meditation, doing some pushups or yoga, journaling, etc.). If you start by trying to quit a bad habit, you're setting yourself up for failure.

Second, when you start a new habit, make a huge commitment (public accountability, a big consequence) . . . but make the habit small. As small as you can. Meditate for just two minutes, but make it incredibly embarrassing if you fail two days in a row, for example.

So don't overdo the habit, but commit big.

Chapter 12

Accountability and Unmissable Consequences

Accountability with consequences has been one of the most effective techniques in getting me to push through resistance. It's worked for some of my biggest goals:

- When I ran my first marathon, I wrote about it every two weeks in my local newspaper, and people from all over Guam (where I lived) cheered me on for an entire year as I trained. I finished that marathon.

- When I ran my first (and only) 50-mile ultramathon, I trained with my friend Scott—having the accountability of him waiting for me for long training runs guaranteed that I'd be there. We finished that run.

- Once I did a diet challenge where my friend Tynan promised, if I didn't stick to the challenge, to throw a pie in my face, record it on video, and post it online. I knew that I'd never let that happen, and I stuck with the challenge for six months.

- I've done pushup and sketching challenges with my

family, where we all did the challenge every day for a month and reported in to each other.

- I've had group challenges with friends where we report in every day via a Google Spreadsheet, so we can all see each others' progress (or lack thereof). Some of those challenges had rewards and negative consequences.

Those are just a few examples, but I've used variations on these ideas many times over the last 10 years, with lots of success.

Every time I think accountability (and big consequences) would help me stick to a habit or goal, I find a way to make it happen. Here are some variations on these ideas that might be helpful:

- **Challenges with a group**: This is one of my favorite ways of setting up accountability. People seem to love to say yes to group challenges. Set up a way to report every day (a shared online spreadsheet, Facebook, email, etc.). Embarrassing consequences for failing, or a big reward at the end of the challenge, are helpful. A good length of a challenge is 2–3 weeks, or a month at the longest.

- **Accountability partner**: Having a running or workout partner has helped me stick to exercise over the years. Just knowing that my sister (my running partner at the time) was going to be waiting in the cold and darkness at 5 A.M. if I didn't get out of bed to join her for a run is enough of a push for me, and would be for most people.

- **Peer group**: I check in with peers every week to let them know how my work projects are going. I just start a weekly email thread every Monday, and we all report in. And it's helpful to know that support is there. Some people like to check in via video chat every week or two.

- **Big public commitment**: Tell everyone you know, online or off, about your commitment to your habit. Ask them to check in on you. Set a big consequence for not checking in and sticking with your habit.

- **A class or in-person group**. A meditation group is a great way to stick to meditating regularly. A drawing or language class will help you practice activities like that regularly. You don't just practice when the class or group meets—you often will practice between classes as well.

- **Online forum**: If you can't do any of the above, find an online forum of other people trying to do the same thing as you. I found a smoking cessation group online when I was quitting smoking and it helped a lot to connect with people who were going through the same thing as me, who'd had some success and knew what worked. I promised them that I wouldn't smoke without posting on the forum first, and that commitment was helpful. I've used online forums to support my running habit, weight loss, and more.

If none of the above work for you, just find one person you trust, and ask them to hold you accountable. Report to them daily. Set a consequence for not checking in or sticking to what you're committed to doing.

Accountability works because as humans, we're social animals. We don't like to look bad in the eyes of our peers, and we like to look good. So if we're a part of a group, we'll do our best to stick to something.

Consequences work because we don't want to embarrass ourselves, so we'll do whatever we can to avoid the consequences. You should make the consequence as embarrassing as possible, so you definitely won't let it happen—I call this an "unmissable consequence" because it's so strong I definitely won't miss doing my habit. And you should make the habit so easy you will definitely do it every single day, no matter what.

Chapter 13

Facing Resistance with Mindfulness

Resistance comes up for every habit—for every difficult task we set before ourselves, actually. Our usual response is to run from that resistance.

It's a mental habit that we all have very strongly ingrained in us: we tend to avoid even thinking about the resistance.

Think about the last time you skipped doing a habit (or a difficult task like a report) for a couple days—most likely, you didn't even want to think about that habit. You felt guilty, you dreaded thinking about the habit, so you distracted yourself with other things. You put off dealing with it or even thinking about it until later.

We all do this. Faced with resistance, we run. This has the consequence of making things more difficult for us, unfortunately. When we avoid thinking about the exercise habit or eating healthy, our health becomes worse. We avoid thinking about finances or clutter and those just pile up. We avoid thinking about our habits of distraction and procrastination and those make our lives more difficult.

So what's the alternative to running? **Facing the resistance with mindfulness**.

Instead of avoiding, actually turn to the resistance. Look it in the face. Try to really see it. Be curious about it: what is it like? How does it feel in your body? What kind of energy does it have and where is it located, physically? What effects is it causing in you and your life?

When we turn towards the resistance, we are making the courageous decision to stay with it, to accept that it's there, to work with it instead of rejecting it.

Try this—notice what resistance you've had lately (anything you've procrastinated on). And turn towards it for just a minute:

1. See that you've been resisting.

2. See what story you've been telling yourself about that resistance. What rationalizations do you have for procrastinating?

3. See how the resistance feels, physically, in your body. Be curious about it, and see it with a friendly gaze.

4. Notice the stress in your body that results from the resistance.

5. Send compassion, love, friendliness to this feeling of stress, to the resistance you're feeling.

It takes practice. This is a compassionate act, a friendly act. It's like telling a friend, "Hey, I'm not going to run from you when you're having difficulty, I'm going to stay with you, listen to you, give you a hug, give you love." Except that instead of a friend, it's ourselves.

Practice working with your resistance in this friendly way, and see if you are then freed to act despite the resistance.

You can feel the resistance, turn towards it, send compassion towards it, and then do the habit despite the resistance.

Chapter 14

The Just Get Started Mindset

One of the tricks that helped me start the running habit was so simple you'd think it wouldn't work. The trick was to tell myself that **all I had to do was lace up my shoes and get out the door**. That's all I had to do.

It worked. That was such a simple habit that I couldn't really say no to it. I laced up my shoes, got out the door, and then inevitably I would start running. I didn't have to run far, just start moving . . . but once I started moving, going a little further was an easy proposition.

I learned from this experience that **the most important moment of any habit is the moment of starting**. That's because if you don't start, you're not doing the habit. And lots of us put off the moment of starting, so that we don't do the habit at all.

So just get started. Tell yourself that all you have to do each day is just start the habit. Just start.

Some examples:

- If you're going to meditate, all you have to do is get your butt on the cushion.

- If your habit is sketching, just put your pencil on the paper.

- If your habit is writing, just write the first sentence.

- If your habit is doing yoga, just start with child's pose.

- If your habit is lifting weights, just do the first warmup set.

- If your habit is eating healthier, just have one bite of a vegetable.

- If your habit is flossing, just floss one tooth.

It's that simple. Focus on the moment of starting, tell yourself you don't have to do anything else, and then do that one moment with the intention of love.

Chapter 15

Rule: Don't Miss Two Days

I've found that one of the biggest pitfalls when you're trying to create a new habit is when you start missing days. If you've got a good habit streak going, everything is great . . . until you miss a day or two.

When you miss a day, the mind seems to dislike the breaking of the streak. All the good feelings you had about getting a good streak going are now turned into disappointment and guilt. You feel like you let yourself down.

And what does the mind do as a result of these bad feelings? It avoids even thinking about the habit. If you remember that you're supposed to do the habit, you are likely to turn away from thinking about it, push it back into the deep recesses of your mind.

This problem compounds if you keep missing days, until you don't want to think about the habit at all.

Missing one day doesn't seem to be a big problem, although it's not the best. Sometimes missing a day is unavoidable—you get sick, you have a visitor, a crisis comes up. But if you can avoid missing two days, you should.

So here's the rule you might try sticking to: b.

If you miss a day, no problem, just start again the next

day. But do everything you can to not miss two days. Write it down, ask someone for help, set some consequences. Actually, setting a big embarrassing consequence for missing two days in a row is a great idea.

If you don't miss two days in a row, you're much more likely to stick to the habit. And you'll learn that it's not a big deal to miss a day, as long as you get back on it.

Wanting to Give up after Missing a Day

A common issue is missing a day of your habit, and then wanting to give up.

The rule of "never missing two days in a row" helps with this, because you anticipate missing a day now and then . . . but you're committed to not letting that ruin your habit. You know that the habit won't go perfectly, and will have disruptions . . . but you're practicing starting again as soon as you get disrupted.

What if you want to give up? Ask for help. Ask a friend to stop you from giving up. Talk to them (or journal) about why you're feeling like giving up. Dig into your resistance, face it with mindfulness, and then remind yourself of your deeper motivation.

Chapter 16

Distractions

Here's a common scenario: you plan to do your habit, and then you face distractions from things online or from people around you.

How do you overcome distractions and focus on doing the habit?

First, it's good to become aware that you're being distracted. See that you intended to do the habit but then got pulled away. What are your biggest distractions? What are you running from?

Second, be mindful of your resistance, as we discussed in a previous chapter. Stay with it instead of running to distractions.

Third, ask others for help. If it's distracting with people around, ask those people to push you to do your habit even when you're around.

Fourth, change your environment. Get away from others when you need to do your habit (if possible). Close your browser and email program if you are trying to journal (for example). Whatever your distractions are, shut them down or go somewhere that they're not a problem, to make things easier on you.

Fifth, set up strong consequences and accountability if needed. It will help you overcome the resistance and distractions.

Chapter 17

Overcoming Disruptions like Illness and Travel

It's a fact of life: we all get sick sometimes. Also, many of us need to travel several times during the year. Or we have a family crisis, a huge work project takes all our waking hours, a loved one gets sick, or we have visitors to our homes.

These are some of the more common habit disruptions. And we can't always control the disruptions, so learning to deal with them is an essential habit skill.

There are two ways I suggest dealing with these kinds of common disruptions, and either will work:

1. **Anticipate and adjust**. If you know that you're going to have a visitor, or you're traveling, or a big project is coming up that will change your schedule . . . anticipate this change in advance and see if you can change your habit so that you can still do it. For example, get up a little earlier and meditate in a different room if a visitor is disrupting your usual meditation schedule and location. Or set extra reminders to do your habit in your hotel room if you're traveling. However, you can't always anticipate disruptions—getting sick or

having a family crisis aren't predictable. So then try the next method.

2. **Restart as soon as possible**. When you get disrupted, then you simply need to start again as soon as you can. When you notice you're getting disrupted (you come down with a cold, for example), simply let the habit go for the moment, and set a reminder to restart your habit to go off in a few days. When the illness or trip or crisis is over, recommit yourself and simply start again. Don't let it become a big deal that you got disrupted—just restart.

Disruptions don't have to be the end of the world. Just be a little more mindful when they happen, and either adjust or start again when the disruption is over. Treat them like small bumps in the road, and take them in stride.

Chapter 18

Overcoming a Slump

Let's say you don't succeed at the previous rule ("Don't Miss Two Days in a Row"), or you give in to distractions, or you get disrupted by illness . . . and you fall into a bit of a slump. You've missed a few days, maybe a week or more . . . and you don't even want to think about the habit.

This slump is often the ending of a new habit. We don't think about the habit, feel guilty about it, and put it off until we've completely given up.

So if you're in a slump, this is a crucial juncture: are you going to just give up, or are you going to get out of the slump?

This is a key habit skill—getting yourself out of that slump.

How do we do it? I've been in many slumps myself, and though I'm not perfect, I've broken out of some of them. Here's what I've found to be helpful:

1. **Recognize that you're in a slump**. Be honest with yourself.

2. **Ask for help**. Get a friend to help give you the accountability and support that you need to get started again.

3. **Start super small**. Just the smallest thing you can do to get going again.

4. **Celebrate that tiny success**. Reflect on how you got started again, after taking that super small step. Tell your friend about it, and celebrate.

5. **Set a consequence**. Tell yourself and your friend that you're going to do the super small step every day for the next week, with a consequence for missing a day.

Get help, start small, and get moving again. That's all it takes, and it's not that hard, but if you don't put in the effort and focus that's required, your habit will die.

Chapter 19

Create the Right Environment

If resistance is the reason we struggle with habits, and our minds want to just run away from resistance, are we just doomed to fail?

Yes. In normal circumstances, we will fail because of the power of resistance and the power of the mind to run from resistance. However, *in the right environment*, we can actually overcome that resistance.

Sometimes we just happen to have the right environment. For example, if you're in the military, you're much more likely to exercise and keep a neat bed, because 1) there are people who tell you to and are checking up on you, 2) you look good among your peers if you excel at these things, and 3) you're likely to get punished if you don't do those habits.

Lots of other environments are well-suited to helping us overcome resistance. When I was working at a daily newspaper, I overcame the resistance to writing and wrote articles every day, because of the environment. I wrote more fiction when I was in a writing group, trained for a marathon when I was in a running group (or when I had a running partner), studied more when I was in college.

But what if you're not in the right environment? You'll know you're not if you are constantly struggling with productivity, health or mindfulness habits. **The good news is: we can create the right environment.**

A lot of examples are found in this book. Think about some of the following things you can do to set up a good environment:

- Create accountability with other people.

- Set up consequences and rewards.

- Set up reminders—digital and physical.

- Get rid of the junk food in your house and have only healthy food.

- Set up a challenge so that you and others can support each other.

- Join a group or a class.

- Get a coach.

- Allow others to see what you're doing, so you're less likely to cheat.

- Make the habit small and the motivation strong.

- Join an online forum or group to support your habit.

Those are just some examples—what can you think of to make your environment more conducive to the habit you're trying to form?

It's a good habit skill to consider your environment, see how it might be helping or hurting your habit, and then changing the environment in small or big ways to help you succeed rather than fail.

Chapter 20

Practice the Skill of Mindfulness

When you're doing a habit, like exercise for example, it's easy to get into the mode of "just get it over with." It's like a chore you have to do, a task you have to check off your to-do list.

But this is a mistake. If the habit is like a chore that you need to finish, then it becomes something you dislike, are bored with, even dread. And there's only so long you'll keep up a habit like that, in my experience.

What if, instead, it was something you enjoyed? What if you looked forward to this beautiful break in your busy day?

The skill of mindfulness can help with this. It's about being present with the habit, paying attention, finding things to appreciate about it, finding joy in each step instead of looking forward to some goal in the future.

Here's how I recommend practicing:

1. Notice when you're feeling rushed and looking towards other things you have to do after the habit.

2. Pause, and think about your intention with this habit. If you're doing it out of love for other people, for example, bring this love into the doing of the habit.

3. Try to pay attention to your body, your movement, and your surroundings as you do the habit.

4. When your mind wanders to something else, just notice and gently bring it back.

5. Be curious about what's happening right now, in the present moment, as you do the habit. What does it feel like? What can you discover?

6. What can you find to appreciate and be grateful for right now?

7. Smile, breath, do the habit slowly, and enjoy yourself right now. Treat this like a spa break.

You don't have to do all of that at once, but you can pick two or three things on this list to practice with. Eventually you'll get better at these skills and won't need to think of the list, but it's good to come back to it as a reminder, because mindfulness is something that's easy to forget as we rush through our day.

Chapter 21

Journaling and Reflecting

One of the most powerful tools for creating a habit is reflection. And journaling is one of the best ways to reflect regularly. So the habit of journaling is one of the best habits you can form to help form all other habits.

Why is reflection so important? Because it's a way of reviewing how you're doing, what's going right, and what's going wrong. You can see the obstacles that are getting in the way, and figure out how to overcome them. You can reflect on the resistance you've been feeling, and pick one of the techniques in this book to overcome it.

Basically, it's the opposite of what causes most people to fail: not only do we face resistance that causes us to struggle, but we avoid even thinking about that resistance. **This avoidance is the real cause of our failure**. If we don't avoid thinking about the resistance, we can figure out how to overcome it. This is what reflection does for us.

There are lots of ways to reflect on your habit regularly. One of my favorite ways is to reflect during a walk or a run. Get away from everything else, no headphones and no music or audiobooks, just yourself and your thoughts.

As you're forced to be alone with yourself for a little while, reflection becomes a natural activity.

You can also just have a reminder at the end of each day to pause for a few minutes to reflect on how the day went. You could email someone with reflections on your day or your week. Or you could journal.

Journaling can be made easy: just commit to writing a few sentences every day. A five-sentence journal only has to take one or two minutes. If you feel moved to write more than five sentences, great! Go for it. Otherwise, just meet the minimum requirement, and reflect for a moment each day on how your day has gone (or how yesterday went, if you're journaling in the morning).

As you reflect, think about what you did right—and take a moment to celebrate that! It reinforces what you want to do by rewarding yourself with self-praise.

Think also about how you might have failed. Failure in this case is nothing to feel bad about, but rather it's useful information. You can use this information to self-correct, change what you're doing. What can you add to your method or your environment to make it more likely you'll stay on the right path? Make a note to implement that immediately.

Reflection is an easy habit, but a powerful one. I highly recommend it in any habit creation effort.

Chapter 22

Don't Rely on Feeling Like It

When we're thinking about whether we're going to do our habit (or any task, really), the most common criteria people use is: do I feel like it right now?

This is a mistake. If you're feeling tired, not in a good mood, rushed, overwhelmed, uncertain, uncomfortable, uninspired, unmotivated . . . you'll skip the habit.

Don't rely on your mood to determine whether or not to do a habit.

Don't rely on "feeling like it."

Instead, figure out beforehand if you're going to do the habit or not. The day before, the week before, but not right in the moment when you're supposed to do it.

If you plan to meditate when you wake up, don't put the question to yourself in the morning. You'll be tired then! You won't feel like it. Instead, plan the day before to meditate when you wake up . . . then when you wake up, just do it.

If you plan to work out after work, when you're done with work, don't even ask the question. Just do the workout.

How do you get yourself to do the habit when you don't feel like it? Don't let it be a question. Just say, "OK it's time, now let's do it." Get in the habit of not asking, just get moving. Just start, without asking.

Yes, this is contrary to how we normally do things. But how we normally do things doesn't work, not when it comes to habits or beating procrastination. Not when we're faced with resistance.

Instead, change things up. Just start, without asking the question.

Chapter 23

Don't Talk Yourself Out of It

I have a friend who makes serious plans for his future, gets excited about the plans . . . and then when push comes to shove, he gets doubts. A week or two later, he's making up completely new plans for the future.

What happened? He talked himself out of his plans.

This is something we all do—when things are tough or uncertain, we have lots of doubts. We rationalize why we should back out. But it's such a pattern with my friend that I called him out on it: "Stop talking yourself out of it," I said to him.

Now, whenever he starts to back out, I remind him, "You're talking yourself out of it again!" And he admits he is. We have an agreement that he has to redouble his focus and efforts on his original plans when this happens, really try to take action.

Again, we all do it. We have a plan for what we're going to do for today, and then when we have to do it . . . we talk ourselves out of it.

Some excuses we make:

- I'm tired.

- I don't feel like it (not in the mood).

- I deserve a break.

- One more Youtube video won't hurt.

- I'll just check email real quick first.

- I don't know if this is going to work—I should think of something else.

- Those dishes need washing instead!

- I can't do this, I should just quit.

- This is too hard, I hate this, I don't know what I was thinking.

Those are just some examples—you probably have your own set of rationalizations, right? What do you say to talk yourself out of what you planned to do?

The trick is to realize that you're rationalizing, that you're talking yourself out of it. **And then don't let yourself talk yourself out of it**.

Talk yourself into it instead.

Chapter 24

Getting through the Dip

The first year that I started changing my life by changing my habits, I discovered something really interesting happened after about 2–3 weeks into a new habit.

I would consistently hit a dip in motivation at 2–3 weeks. I started calling it The Dip (in homage to Seth Godin, who wrote a book for entrepreneurs with that title).

The Dip, when it comes to habits, comes after the initial enthusiasm for doing the habit dies down. Here's what typically happens:

1. You start a new habit filled with enthusiasm and ideals about how it will go.

2. You do it for the first week—and if you start as small as possible, as I recommend, you do great!

3. It feels good to be successful the first week, so your enthusiasm pushes into the second week.

4. However, at this point, other things pull at your focus. It's easy to miss a day, or at least not care as much about the habit as you did before.

5. If the habit isn't what you hoped it would be (which is often the case), you feel let down.

6. By the third week, you have lost your initial enthusiasm and focus, and at this point, you're likely to miss 2–3 days of doing the habit.

7. If that happens, your habit is very likely to die.

Yikes! That escalated quickly. But that's a typical pattern, though it varies depending on a lot of factors: what's going on in your life, how much energy you have, how badly the habit fares compared to your hopes, whether you allow yourself to miss two days in a row, etc.

Here's the thing: **if you expect the Dip, you can beat it**. If you know it's coming and plan for it, you can overcome this obstacle.

Some ideas:

- Plan ahead—set a calendar reminder for that week to do a couple things (see next items).

- Ask a friend to give you some extra encouragement and accountability during this period.

- If you miss a day, ask several friends to make sure you don't miss a second day. Set up a seriously embarrassing consequence.

- Get some friends to join you in a challenge.

- If you feel your enthusiasm flagging, try some of the things in this book to get yourself going again. Specifically, tap into your deeper Why once again.

These are some ideas you can try, but the main idea is to expect the Dip and plan for it.

Chapter 25

Restarting and Re-Motivating

It happens to the best of us: we all get stalled on a habit. Things come up, we lose our focus or motivation, life gets in the way.

The question isn't whether or not we'll stop a habit . . . the question is whether we'll start again when that happens.

For example, I recently had my meditation habit stalled (travel and visitors got in the way), and I had trouble starting again. But a few days ago, I started it again, and I'm really glad I did!

So the technique we'll focus on in this chapter is restarting, after getting stalled. And re-motivating ourselves, after losing motivation.

Re-Motivating Ourselves

The first thing is to notice that you're not that motivated anymore. You lost interest, other things came up, you got pumped up about some other thing. When you think of this habit, you just aren't feeling it.

When this happens, it's a red flag—time to figure this out! It's good to go back to your original deeper Why for doing the habit. What moved you to do it in the first place? Can you spend some time thinking more about this motivation and see if you can get moved again?

If you can't even find the motivation to do that, ask a friend for help. It's as simple as sending a quick email or text to a friend saying you need help finding motivation for this habit. When they ask how they can help, ask for some accountability, some encouragement, setting consequences, talking over the deeper Why. This is tremendously helpful.

Look for other reasons to get excited as well. Talk yourself into doing this.

Restarting When We're Stalled

If you've stopped doing the habit altogether, this is another red flag. Unfortunately, we often don't even want to think about the habit when we've stopped doing it, so it can be a problem even noticing the red flag when we've given up.

The solution, again, is to phone a friend. Or email them. Ask for help. You might even ask them to keep you honest before you stall with the habit, when you're just getting started, in anticipation of stalling. Ask them to check in with you every few days to see if you're still sticking with it.

If you're stalled, getting motivation as in the previous section is a great idea. But **re-starting as small as possi-**

ble is the best prescription—for example, I re-started my meditation habit recently by just sitting for a minute or two. Lower the friction for re-starting.

And as in the previous chapter, you can ask friends to join you in a new challenge, or set up an embarrassing consequence and ask friends to hold you to it, to get started again.

The main takeaway is that you can always re-start if you get stalled, and re-starting is actually a key skill in forming habits. Start small, get some motivation, and get going again! Don't let stopping become a big deal—it's just a bump in the road.

Chapter 26

On Consistency

Consistency with a habit is something people struggle with the most. It can be a difficult thing, but we've covered the most important ideas when it comes to being consistent—I'd like to just take a moment to review a few of them:

1. **Small habits**. If you keep the habit as small as possible (just 2 minutes, for example), then it's much easier to be consistent.

2. **One at a time**. Trying to form multiple habits at once makes it harder to be consistent. One habit at a time makes it much easier.

3. **Motivation and accountability**. If you have a deeper motivation and strong accountability, you're more likely to be consistent.

4. **Dealing with resistance**. Resistance (and the procrastination that results) is the main reason we stop doing a habit. Learn to deal with the resistance using the techniques I presented earlier in this book, and you'll stay on track more often.

5. **Just getting started mentality**. When it's time to do the habit, just start, as simply as possible. This is another way of dealing with the resistance.

6. **Getting back on track**. No one is perfect at the habit—there are disruptions, we miss a day—but if we can get good at just getting started again, we can be more consistent rather than less consistent. Get back on track after disruptions.

These are the key habit skills when it comes to developing consistency. If you can work on these skills, along with some of the other ideas in this book, you'll develop a greater consistency over time.

However, it's good to note that you don't have to ever be "perfect" with a habit. We'll all face bumps in the road, and some habits just won't stick the first try (or even the second or the third). For example, meditation is one habit that I have started and stopped many times over the years—and yet, I keep coming back to it, because I find it immensely helpful. I'm not perfect at it by any means, but I'm OK with that.

We can get better at consistency, but we'll never be completely, perfectly consistent. In the end, just keep coming back.

Chapter 27

Overcoming Adversity

Our lives are never perfect . . . and neither are we. So when we face difficulties, moments of weakness, stress, it's natural that we're not perfect with our habits.

Getting better at how we deal with the adversity can help us be better at habits. So let's look at a few situations.

1. **Moments of weakness.** We all have those moments, when we're tempted by something or not feeling very strong willed. In that moment, if you can pause instead of procrastinating on the habit or giving in to temptation, that is a incredibly useful skill. Just pause, and notice your rationalizations, notice your urge, stay with it instead of just acting on it. Reflect on your intention or motivation behind this habit. Give yourself a chance to choose to do the habit. If you give in to the weakness, instead of being harsh with yourself, be kind, let it go, and start again. The starting again is more important than self-criticism.

2. **Difficult or stressful times**. When things get tough, it's easy to skip the habit because we're stressed out or not feeling up to doing the habit. First, pause and be mindful of your stress level, your sense of loss,

your frustrations . . . anything that's difficult for you right now. Give yourself some compassion. Next, think about how your habit will actually be helpful in this moment of difficulty, and see if you can do a reduced version of it, just to keep it going. Third, if the habit isn't helpful right now, consider taking a break until things calm down. Set a reminder for later and get started again as soon as you're able. Sometimes you have to make room for difficult times.

3. **Overwhelmed by other things and dropping habits**. We often get overwhelmed by all we have to do. However, dropping all our helpful habits isn't always the answer. Again, it's OK to take a break if needed, but if we drop all our habits every time we get overwhelmed, we'll never stick to habits. So, again, it's useful to consider whether you can do a reduced version of the habits, and consider how they might be helpful to you right now. Be mindful of your story about how you're overwhelmed and don't have time for the habits, and see if you can instead take some time to meditate, do your habits, and not feel you need to do everything all at once.

4. **Doing habits when it's harder (tired, it's late, etc.)**. In those moments of being tired, it's easy to skip the habit. And if you're super exhausted, that's OK. Just do it again the next day. But you might also consider whether you're just rationalizing, and whether you can do the habit anyway, or at least a very minimal version of it. Learning to do the habit when tired is an amazing skill that will pay off in many ways, not least by reducing your tendency to procrastinate.

As you can see, we have different options when it comes to dealing with our habits during difficult times: we can be mindful and compassionate with ourselves, see our rationalizations, do the habit anyway even if we're tired or stressed; we can do a minimal version of the habit; we can take a break when necessary and just be sure to restart as soon as possible.

These are great habit skills, and you can get better at them with focus and practice.

Chapter 28

Changing Your Identity

As you work with your habits, a technique to practice with is to see how you see yourself.

This view of ourselves is our identity—we might see ourselves as screw-ups, as compassionate, as inadequate, as a lawyer or teacher or writer, as a good mother, as untrustworthy or undisciplined. We have many ways of looking at ourselves, and some of them are unhelpful.

What I've found is that our identity—our view of ourselves—can actually get in the way of forming new habits.

For example:

- If you see yourself as a smoker, then it's hard to give up smoking—it's a key part of how you see yourself and feel about yourself.

- If you see yourself as a meat eater and someone who loves cheese, then it would be hard to eat a vegan diet.

- If you see yourself as someone who hates exercise or vegetables, then it's hard to make those changes.

- If you don't see yourself as a "meditator" then it's hard to meditate regularly. And in fact, you might see yourself as a "bad meditator" and so meditating is frustrating for you.

As you can see, identity can be an obstacle. However, the good news is that **identity can also be helpful—and it's also changeable!**

I changed my identity from a "meat eater" to a "vegan" and now a vegan diet is not only my default way of eating, I see it as an integral part of my way of life.

I changed my identity from someone who was sedentary and bad at sticking to exercise . . . to a marathoner and eventually someone who loves working out.

I changed my identity to someone who meditates regularly, to someone who is a patient and loving father, to someone who writes every day, to someone who lives minimally.

And yes, in some cases I don't completely live up to those ways of seeing myself, but in the end, I always go back to them because I've changed how I think of myself.

So yes, identity can be changed. I recommend you change it consciously—start calling yourself a "regular meditator" or an "ex-smoker" or a "habitual exerciser" or something like that. Journal about it, repeat it to yourself, and start to view everything you do through that lens. Soon, your identity won't be getting in the way, but will actually make you stick to your desired changes.

Chapter 29

Dealing with Negative Thinking

It's a fact of life that we have negative thoughts. In fact, we can get locked into negative thinking, self-judgment, and harshness . . . and this can be a big obstacle to changing habits.

If we don't think we can do it, we probably won't. If we think the habit sucks, we probably won't stick with it for long. If we complain about how tired or stressed we are, we'll probably skip the habit because it's too hard to do it right now.

We might think, "I suck at this, I'm weak and undisciplined, I can't do this, I never stick to anything." In some ways, this is because we have an identity of never sticking to anything (see the previous chapter). But in other ways, it's because we're allowing this negative thinking to control our lives. We're letting the self-judgment stop us.

So how do we get out of this? It's not always easy, I'll admit, so it's good to be forgiving of ourselves if we slip up in this area.

Here's what I recommend:

- **Notice when you're being judgmental of yourself,**

or stuck in negative thinking. Just see it happening. Journaling can help with this.

- **Just acknowledge it with gentleness and a sense of humor**: "Ah, I'm doing it again," you might say with a smile.

- **Notice the difficult feeling in your body**—not your thoughts about it, but the physical feeling. How does it feel? Stay with the physical feeling for a minute.

- **Have compassion for this feeling**—a loving feeling of not wanting to have this stress in your body. Send yourself a warm, loving feeling.

- **Change the story**: instead of saying that you suck or can't do it, instead of saying that the habit sucks . . . say that you're doing something great just by attempting it. You're building trust in yourself. You're trying to do something good for others. You are grateful for the opportunity to practice with this. You appreciate the moment as you're doing it. These stories are helpful.

The truth is, we all have these moments of judgment and negativity. It's OK. It doesn't mean anything bad about us. Instead, we can acknowledge our difficulty, and see if we can be compassionate about it and find a way to appreciate the love we have as we're trying to create a new habit.

Chapter 30

Habit Questions and Other Struggles

In this chapter, I thought I'd address questions and common habit struggles submitted by readers.

1. **Implementing habits despite depression or anxiety or ADHD.** Unfortunately these three conditions make it difficult to form new habits. Acknowledge this, and start small and don't try to form too many. Habits such as meditation, exercise and journaling can be very helpful for these conditions, so focus on those habit first, and see them as a way to help yourself through difficulties.

2. **I struggle with juggling new habits with family schedules, having toddlers, lots of work.** It's good to acknowledge that it's difficult to find the room for new habits when you have so much going on. But also acknowledge that there is probably a little wiggle room—time you spend watching TV or browsing the Internet or social media on your phone, for example. You can sacrifice a little of this for the habit you most want to form—if it's important, you can make the time.

Keep the habit very small, and you'll be able to make the small amount of room you need. Don't form too many at once; make it a very gradual process because you already have a lot going on. And create habits that are helpful for making more space, like waking a little earlier or picking a couple tasks to focus on each morning.

3. **Changes in physical environment mess up my triggers**. You've realized that triggers are completely dependent on your physical environment, which is an important realization. So if you have a changing physical environment, like if you travel a lot, you'll need to have a way to remember to put physical reminders in your new environment. I suggest planning ahead each week, so you can look at what will be changing and set calendar and phone reminders. When you get the phone reminder, put a physical note or object to remind you in your new environment (like your running shoes next to your bed in your hotel room). Also ask someone to remind you if you need it.

4. **How do I recover a good habit that I lost?** Acknowledge that you have fallen out of the habit, and that you want to get back into it. Spend a minute thinking about your deeper motivation, your trigger, and your commitment and accountability. Then start again, simply and as small as possible. Just get started again, without criticizing yourself for stopping. Put some focus into it for a month, so that it becomes more automatic, but be mindful of when you get disrupted or feel like skipping it.

5. **When can I add additional habits to the mix?** Slowly. When the first habit becomes more and more automatic, consider adding a second habit but starting small and not increasing the first habit much. Keep

both small so you can fit them into your life. Repeat the process with the third habit, but add only very gradually. I would give each habit at least a month of full focus before adding another. Six weeks would be even better if you can find the patience.

6. **I get bored with my rate of progress**. That's because we're impatient to get all of our habits done. But it's an ineffective way of forming habits, so stick with the gradual method. You didn't form your current habits overnight—it took years. So expect new habits to take time as well. If you're bored, use each day's habit as a form of meditation, trying to pay close attention to every detail, focusing on the fun of doing it and learning in the moment. There's a lot to learn, if you pay attention. Alternatively, do the habit socially—go for a walk with a friend, meditate with others, join a group challenge.

7. **I have a hard time with habits I dislike, like exercise and studying**. The problem is seeing them as something you dislike. Change your story about them— see them as a great learning process, a way to love yourself, a way to make you better able to help others. Do them in small bits at first, so they're not too uncomfortable. Find things to appreciate about the moment as you do them. Add a social component to make them more enjoyable.

8. **After building a new habit every day for a few months, I tend to revert to old habits again**. It's good to be aware of this tendency. When you find yourself starting to revert, ask people for help. Get some accountability going, make the habit smaller if needed, add a social component or some challenge to make it more fun. And remind yourself of your deeper motivation, so you'll want to keep doing it.

9. **How do I stick to habits on weekends (when my kids are around all day)?** You can either skip them on weekends if it's too difficult, or find a way to get your kids involved, or find some space (like in the early mornings or evenings) where you can do them without interruptions. Put some extra focus and reminders and accountability on weekends so you don't forget.

10. **How do I move from intentional practice to effortlessly integrating?** Slowly. Things become more and more automatic with time, and eventually you don't have to think about it much. But intentional practice is a really good thing, so don't rush through it. Find gratitude and appreciation each time you do the habit, and do it with love.

11. **How do I find the balance between making the habit important and not obsessive?** Great question! It's very useful to make the habit important—if you have a deeper motivation, then it's definitely worth putting some focus into it. But it's also useful to be mindful of a tendency to over focus, to overcommit, to over obsess. If you find yourself doing that, pause, breathe, and take a step back. See that you're getting too lost in the weeds, too lost in your ideals about the habit. See if there's something else you can put your focus on for the rest of the day, and only put your focus on the habit at the appropriate time.

12. **I struggle with believing deeply that I deserve the good that changing habits can bring.** See the chapter on Changing Your Identity—you see yourself as someone who isn't worthy of good changes. Instead, start to form an identity of a good person who loves herself or himself, who wants good changes and is willing to put in the loving work to make them stick. Yes, this will take some time, but you can make this change. Ask for help from others in your life if needed.

13. **What I'd really like to know is what is the end-game, the payoff? Why even bother with habits?** We can go through life mindlessly, and it would be a waste of the gift we've been given. We can go through life thinking it's not worth much, but that would be a waste, not appreciating the beauty in front of us. In the end, I think life is filled with goodness, filled with small joys, if we just pay attention. In this way, forming habits is a conscious, intentional way of living, and being mindful is the way of seeing the goodness in life.

Part II

QUITTING A HABIT, COMMON HABITS

In this section of the book, I'm going to go into three areas:

1. Quitting bad habits, which is a more complicated habit skill than forming a new habit.

2. Other types of habits like irregular habits, which are also a bit more complicated.

3. Common habits that a lot of people want to form.

The bulk of this section will be about specific habits that lots of people are interested in creating. I don't go into a lot of depth on any of them, but just share some notes for each. You'll see that a lot of the ideas we've already talked about can be applied to these specific habits.

Chapter 31

Overview of Quitting a Bad Habit

Forming a new, positive habit is the basic habit method I recommend in this book, because it's the easiest version of habit change. Start with the basic method first, before moving on to harder techniques like quitting a bad habit.

However, eventually you'll want to quit a bad habit—smoking, junk food, chewing your nails, drinking too much, watching YouTube too much, etc. So let's talk about that.

But you should be aware that this is a big topic, and I'm only going to touch on these topics briefly here.

When You're Ready to Quit

First hone your habit-forming skills by forming several new, positive habits before trying to quit a bad habit. But you know you're ready to quit *when you have a very strong desire to quit*, and are willing to put in the hard work and time needed to quit a habit. You should have a very strong reason to quit, a deeper motivation. It's not easy, so you have to be willing to put up with strong urges, with rationalizations, and with lots of doubts about whether you should be doing this or not.

Gradual Vs. Cold Turkey

When I quit smoking, I quit cold turkey. I set a quit date two weeks in the future, and counted down the days until that date. I used the two weeks until my quit date to prepare by listing my triggers and coming up with replacement habits (see sections below). Then when my quit date came, I told myself, "Not one puff ever!" And I didn't smoke again (though it was quite a struggle). If you're going to do it this way, I recommend a nicotine replacement patch, which I didn't use myself.

However, that is a pretty difficult way to quit, and many psychologists recommend a more gradual method. For example, you might smoke fewer cigarettes per day at first, and gradually wean yourself off cigarettes one step at a time. If you want to quit junk food, you might slowly replace your junk snacks with whole foods (like fruit and carrots and raw unsalted nuts).

I recommend the gradual method, but it does take longer. That means you have to have a long view, and some patience. If you don't have the patience, and think you can muster the courage to go cold turkey, give it a try . . . but be ready to also try the gradual method if you don't make cold turkey work.

Listing Your Triggers

I recommend spending a few days making tally marks on a piece of paper every time you do your bad habit or get the urge to do your bad habit. Carry a pen and paper around and try to catch the urge as often as you can, making a tally mark and also writing down what triggered the urge (eating, stress, being around others who smoke, being at a bar, etc.).

By making tally marks, you're developing an awareness of the urge. By making a list of triggers, you're starting to see what triggers the urge, and taking the first step in making a plan to find replacement habits. Be prepared to add other triggers to your list later, as you discover new ones you didn't find at first.

Coping and Finding Replacement Habits

Your bad habit actually serves a purpose—it helps you cope with stresses. Those stresses might include feeling lonely, angry, frustrated, depressed, hurt, anxious, over-whelmed, and so on. This is a useful purpose, but obviously the bad habit isn't a great method for coping with these stresses because it causes other problems, and those problems themselves cause more stress.

So a key part of quitting a bad habit is finding other ways to cope with stresses. Those might include mindfulness and meditation, taking a bath, having tea, going for a walk, exercising, doing yoga, getting a massage (or massaging yourself), talking to someone, simplifying your schedule, or other strategies.

And an important strategy is to find a replacement habit for each trigger on your list from the section above. If the trigger is "getting into an argument," then you should find a positive replacement habit for coping with the stress of an argument—perhaps meditation or going for a walk, instead of smoking.

Make a list with a replacement habit for each trigger, and see if you can start to form these new habits very consciously from now on.

Getting The Support

Creating new habits and fighting the urges to go to the old habit won't be the easiest thing in the world. It's good to have others who support your efforts. Ask the important people in your life for help, commit to them and ask for accountability. Promise to tell them when you're struggling with an urge, and ask for some kind of help from them when that happens.

If you don't have anyone in your life you can ask for support, look to online forums for help. There are lots of people going through what you're going through, and you can learn from what they've done successfully and how they've overcome difficulties. And ask them for help when you're struggling.

Finding the Willpower

You might find that you really want to change a bad habit, but you just don't seem to have the willpower. It's a big project, after all!

I suggest that you commit yourself to a small change. For example, you might smoke three fewer cigarettes per day (give yourself a cigarette allowance). Or eat fruit as one of your afternoon snacks instead of sweets. Tell others about it, ask for accountability, make a big public challenge with a consequence, and keep the change very small. And remember your deeper reason for wanting to make this change. This means you'll be very motivated but won't have to do too much work. Be all in, and make it easy!

Changing Your Identity

In the end, you have to change how you see yourself. I used to see myself as a "smoker," but that wasn't helpful. So I started seeing myself as a "non-smoker," and that helped a lot. I changed myself from a person who ate junk food to a vegan who ate mostly whole foods, and this shift in identity became an important part of who I am, and made sticking to the changes much easier.

Over the years, I've gone from a disorganized hoarder to a minimalist; from a sedentary person to a marathoner and weight lifter; from a procrastinator to a productive writer; from an impatient dad to a loving father; from a distracted person to a meditator. I'm not perfect at any of these things, but my changes in identity have changed my life.

Chapter 32

Irregular or Frequent Habits

Again, the basic habit method in this book is to create a new, positive habit that happens once per day. That's because it's the easiest kind of habit to form. However, eventually (after 3–5 successful habits, perhaps), you'll want to learn how to form other kinds of habits.

Besides quitting bad habits, there are a few others you might be interested in forming (and note that there is a lot of overlap between these categories):

- **Irregular habits**: These are habits that might occur infrequently and not at regular intervals. For example, you might have the habit of overeating when you go out with friends (maybe a couple times a month?), or responding in anger when you talk about politics with your parents (a few times a year?). The triggers are unpredictable, and might not happen for days, weeks, or even months.

- **More frequent habits**: Lots of habits happen more than once per day. For example, overeating might happen two or three times a day, and getting stuck in email might happen four times a day.

- **Thinking or emotional habits**: This is one of the hardest kind of habits—the way you respond to triggers with emotions or certain kinds of thoughts. For example, you might complain frequently, get frustrated with your spouse or kids, or get angry in traffic. These are difficult because we're often not even aware we're doing them, because they're not physical habits but mental ones. These habits, by the way, might fall into one of the two categories above as well.

- **Continuous habits**: Some habits happen really frequently, throughout the day perhaps. This group has a lot of overlap with the above groups, but it's worth a mention here because I've found they're among the hardest, because you have to be constantly aware. A couple examples: going on social media, constant self-criticism, or resentment/annoyance with other people.

I'm not going to go into detail about how to form these kinds of habits here, but I'll briefly give some ideas for each.

Irregular Habits

If you don't know when a trigger will surface, you have two problems:

1. Remembering to do your replacement habit instead of the old habit; and

2. It will take a longer time to form the new habit as you won't get as many repetitions as a daily habit. For example, in one month, you can get 30 repetitions of a daily habit, and it will become much more automatic at the end of those 30 days . . . but with an irregular habit, if you only get three repetitions in a month, it will take 10 months to get 30 repetitions. Therefore it's harder to form the habit with fewer repetitions.

The solution to the second problem (fewer repetitions) is that you have to wait longer and be more patient. The good news is that you don't have to give it as much focus, and can probably form other habits at the same time.

But remembering to do your replacement habit when the irregular trigger happens is a bigger challenge. If you know ahead of time that the trigger will happen (like when you go out with friends), then it's a good idea to be looking ahead for a few days to a week at a time to see when the trigger might be coming up. Then set a reminder for that day to be on the lookout for the trigger.

If you don't know when the trigger will happen (your spouse giving you a certain tone of voice, for example), then it's an even harder challenge. You will have to look out for your response to that trigger, like rising anger . . . and then try to catch yourself before you respond in anger. Having your spouse support you in this effort, by giving you a gentle sign that you're looking angry, is a good idea. Putting visual reminders where you might be triggered, like your computer for a digital habit, is another good idea.

In the end, this takes a special effort to remember, and you have to expect that you won't always get it right—in which case, it will take even longer to form. Look for gradual improvement rather than immediate success.

More Frequent Habits

The good news with habits that happen more than once a day (say two or three times a day) is that if you're consistent, they can form even faster than once-a-day habits. You might get 30 repetitions of the habit in 10 days, rather than a month.

The challenge is that it's much harder to remember to do

the habit consistently. It takes greater focus and a variety of reminders. Having someone else who can help remind you is a great support. You'll need to be on alert all day, or at least whenever the trigger might possibly happen, so you can try to be more consistent.

However, be forgiving if you forget a lot at first. A good idea is to do an end-of-the-day journal so you review how you did, and therefore even days when you forget can become part of the learning process.

Thinking or Emotional Habits

Most people don't even realize that their emotional reactions, or thinking patterns, are habits. But they are just as much a habit as something physical, like chewing your nails or going for a run. They're just harder to spot because you don't always see what's happening.

Some examples include: negative thinking, self-criticism, complaining, being resentful or annoyed at other people, or responding to someone in frustration or anger.

I don't recommend tackling thinking or emotional habits until you have successfully formed multiple physical habits. But when you're ready, you'll need to commit to greater focus and have lots of reminders (see the tips for "more frequent habits" above).

When you notice a trigger for your emotional response (perhaps someone interrupting you is a trigger for responding in annoyance), you'll want to catch yourself. Have a replacement response ready, and practice doing it.

For example, when someone interrupts you, you might try taking a deep breath, reminding yourself that you love this person, and responding with a smile. You'll need to practice this response very deliberately the first few times, and try very hard to remember. If you start responding in annoyance, simply catch yourself as soon as you can, and try to switch to your new response.

Again, it takes time and patience with yourself to form these kinds of habits, and you shouldn't expect to be perfect at it at all. You'll get better gradually if you give it enough focus.

Continuous Habits

Some habits don't just happen a few times a day, but might happen a dozen times or more throughout the day. The challenge here, of course, is the continued focus and constant remembering you'll have to do.

This is the hardest kind of habit, along with thinking/emotional habits, and I don't recommend trying them until you're fairly proficient at other types of habits.

When you're ready, you'll need as many reminders as you can. You'll want to enlist the help of others to remind you. Put physical reminders everywhere, and perhaps wear a wristband or rubber band as another reminder. Have digital reminders on your phone and computer. Ask for accountability from others. And journal at the end of each day so you're reflecting and learning from your mistakes and successes. Again, a lot of patience is required, and you shouldn't be trying to form other habits at the same time.

Chapter 33

Eating Habits

A lot of people want to lose weight, but they focus on trying out different diets or trying to do crazy amounts of exercise. I find that changing your eating habits is the best route to getting to a healthy weight. It takes awhile to lose weight using this method because habit change is best when gradual, but I've found that it's the best way to achieve lasting health and weight change.

Unfortunately, eating habits can be very tough to change because of a couple of reasons:

1. **Eating is tied to emotional habits**. Many of us turn to comfort food when we feel lonely or sad. We use food for relief when we're tired or stressed. We turn to food when we need love or reward. It can be difficult to change eating habits when food is so tied up in emotional habits.

2. **Food environments are incredibly important and can be difficult to change**. It's hard to resist overeating if we are surrounded by tempting junk food or tempting restaurant food. We are biologically wired to want this food and our unconscious brains will

override our best wishes to eat less or make healthier choices.

3. **Certain foods are fairly addictive**. Sugar, fried foods, pastries or bread, fatty foods, salty snacks, chocolate, and caffeine can all be fairly addictive. Breaking addictions is possible but not always easy.

These problems are not easily solved but they are solvable. We'll go into a few key ideas to help address them.

Gradual Change

Gradual change rather than cold turkey is often the most effective choice. I suggest changing one small thing at a time. Eat some fruits instead of sweets in the afternoon. Add some vegetables to your meals. Eat whole grains instead of refined grains a little at a time.

You can overcome a lot of the hurdles mentioned above by making small changes. It will take a long time to overhaul your entire diet, so have patience. But trying to make wholesale changes all at once is a good recipe for failure for most people.

Emotional Eating

When you rely on food for reward, comfort, love, stress relief, what happens when you just stop eating comfort foods? What would happen if you only ate vegetables and beans, as a hypothetical example? You'd all of a sudden not have a way to address those emotional needs.

So you need to gradually change your coping habits to something healthier. For example, you could use meditation or walking for stress relief, and having a warm bath or hot tea for comfort or reward. This takes a good amount of time, so don't expect to switch suddenly to a healthier diet. Focus first on the coping mechanism while gradually making healthier changes.

Self compassion and learning to love yourself are two incredible habits that are important when it comes to changing emotional eating.

Changing Your Food Environment

One of the most important changes you can make if you want to stop overeating, or to eat healthier food, is changing your food environment. Your food environment is what kind of food you have all around you, how convenient it is, how tempting it is.

For example, one person might have a kitchen pantry and fridge filled with tempting snacks and desserts, fried foods and unhealthy microwave meals. And he or she might go out to eat a lot, and have lots of unhealthy (and tempting) snacks at the office. But another person might have only whole foods at home, with carrots and apples for snacks, and only go out to eat at healthy restaurants. One food environment will inevitably lead to unhealthy choices, the other probably won't.

Slowly clear your house of unhealthy, tempting foods as you try to change your habits. You might need to get your family on board. Or avoid the kitchen as much as possible and have the unhealthy food out of sight, if tossing the unhealthy food is not possible.

Try to get your workplace to either have healthy snacks out in plain sight or hide the unhealthy snacks so they're not as tempting.

Eat out less if possible and try to go to healthier restaurants. Have your healthy options picked before you get there and ask your friends/spouse to hold you to that predetermined choice.

If you have a hard time changing your food environment, do it slowly and try to get others in your life to help you.

Dealing with Food Cravings

We often have food addictions or cravings, such as chocolate or sugar or bread. Cutting them out cold turkey can be very difficult and often we'll struggle with food cravings and even collapse in the face of the cravings.

The answer is not to go cold turkey but to slowly reduce the amount you eat. For example, wean yourself from sugar a little at a time and try to eat whole fruit (not juices) whenever you have sugar cravings.

Chocolate cravings can be met with some 80–85% dark chocolate, weaning yourself down to just a square or two per day.

Salty snack cravings can be met with fresh-popped popcorn with just a little salt, or raw nuts with just a little salt added (not roasted pre-salted nuts). Or carrots and hummus, perhaps.

Find healthier alternatives to meet your cravings, and slowly wean yourself from them.

Mindful Eating

One of the unhealthy habits that leads to overeating is mindless eating. Most of us do this: we watch something or read or talk while we're eating, so that we barely notice the food that's going down our throats. This leads to a lack of awareness of fullness levels, of what kind of food we're eating, of the taste and textures of the food.

In order to change mindless habits, we need to use mindfulness. Put away the book, the phone, the computer, and turn off the TV and any other distractions. Just sit with the food and pay attention as you eat. Notice each bite, chew it slowly, pay attention to textures and smells and sights and tastes. It's a meditation—come back to paying attention when your mind wanders. Eat slowly, put the fork down between bites, take a breath and a sip of water between bites.

You'll notice your food more and perhaps enjoy it more as well. You'll notice your fullness levels more and are less likely to overeat. As you start to appreciate tastes and textures of healthier foods you're trying to switch to, you might even start to like them more.

Mindful eating isn't a complete solution in itself, but can be a part of a mindful movement to healthier eating.

Chapter 34

Exercise Habits

Most people want to form the exercise habit, but have a hard time making it stick. That's because it's engineered wrong, with feedback that makes you not want to do it:

- It's harder than doing things online so you would rather put it off and do the easier, more comfortable tasks.

- It often requires an initial change of clothes, shoes, venue, activity, and mindset—as opposed to switching from writing to email to checking social media sites, which don't require much change at all. So there's a big initial hurdle.

- Many people feel better when they are finished working out than when they are actually doing it, so you're happier when it's over. (Note: Not everyone feels this way—but those who enjoy exercise aren't usually struggling to form the habit.)

So how do we overcome this problem? We address each of those problems by 1) making it easier and more enjoyable, 2) creating social reward for doing the habit, 3) reducing the initial hurdle of doing it.

Start Small

Instead of saying that you need to work out for 30 minutes, try just 10. Or 5 minutes. And don't try to do anything too intense or difficult until you have the habit firmly established.

By making the exercise habit short and easy, you are making it easier to switch from doing things online (for example) to the exercise. You are making it more comfortable instead of uncomfortable. And you're much more likely to think, "Sure, I can just bang out a quick 10-minute run" (or walk or set of pushups, etc.) instead of thinking, "Oh, I don't have the time or energy for that right now, I'll do it later."

Just Get Started

Reduce the initial hurdle to get started by making it as easy as possible. Want to do strength exercises? Drop down near your desk and do some pushups or planks or squats or lunges. Want to run? Put your shoes near your bed, and when you wake up, just put on your shoes and step out the door. Don't think about the entire exercise session (not even if it's only 10 minutes), but the first moment only. Make it as simple and easy to get going as you can, and then just do it.

Make It Social

If you exercise with a friend, it makes it more enjoyable—which means it's more rewarding and you're more likely to keep doing it. Go for a walk with a friend, get a gym or yoga partner, find a group to go running with. When you make it social, you're also much less likely to skip the workout, because you'll have negative feedback for not doing the habit.

When you do the workout with your friend, focus on

enjoying the exercise and conversation. It will help you to keep coming back.

Be Mindful

Lots of people try to tune out their workouts, and if listening to music or podcasts helps get you out the door, then keep doing it if it works. However, I prefer to try to stay mindful of the movement of my body when I work out, as much as I can. That includes running, walking/hiking, lifting weights, cycling, doing yoga, or any other kind of workout.

Why? Because it's an opportunity for me to pay attention and enjoy the moment, which is not something I often do when I'm working or online. In that way, the workout becomes one of my cherished moments of being present, of getting away from my distractions, of appreciating the beauty of my body exerting itself and of everything around me. Instead of tuning out my body's movement, I pay attention to the movement and have learned to love it.

Chapter 35

Discipline, Procrastination, and Motivation Habits

A lot of people submitted their habit struggles in different forms: wanting to be more disciplined, more motivated, less of a procrastinator. In my mind, these are all very related, so I decided to address them together briefly in this chapter.

Let's briefly look at each of these and their relationship to each other:

- **Discipline**. Most people think of discipline as meaning "If I plan to work out and then do my important work tasks before email or social media, then I should stick to that plan." So basically, it's the opposite of procrastinating. If you are procrastinating, you're not disciplined. Let's look at procrastination, then.

- **Procrastination**. We put things off because of resistance, as we talked about in Part I of this book. We went into why we have resistance, and different ideas to overcome it. If we can find ways to overcome resistance with work tasks (and habits), we'll procrastinate less and be more disciplined.

- **Motivation**. This is what gets us over the resistance—
if our motivation is greater than our resistance, we
can stop procrastinating and be more disciplined.

As you can see, all three are essential the same problem
stated in different ways: we face resistance, which causes
us to procrastinate, but if we can find strong enough motivation, we can overcome it and develop better discipline.

Let's briefly look at ideas for all three.

Motivation

What is strong enough motivation to overcome the resistance that's been beating you all these years? Only you can
answer that. You'll have to experiment to see what works
best. But here are some ideas:

- **Pain**: If you've been struggling with various problems
because of procrastination/discipline issues, then not
wanting to hurt yourself in these ways can be a good
motivator. Notice your pain and stress and tell yourself
that you really want to stop making yourself struggle
so much.

- **Love for yourself**: If you want to have a healthier,
more productive, more peaceful, happier life, then
perhaps you'll find motivation in that to overcome
your resistance.

- **Love for others**: If there's something you want to
create that will help others, if your work will make the
lives of other people better, if exercising might inspire
your loved ones to become healthier . . . then this can
be very strong motivation to push through resistance.

- **Social motivation**: If you tell others about the change you want to make, for example, you might be motivated to look good in their eyes, or not embarrass yourself. If you do the activity with others, that can motivate you to show up and do your best. Often being able to share your successes with others can be good motivation, and competitions or fun challenges can also help us push through resistance.

- **Accountability**: This is specific a form of social motivation—you say you're going to do something, you promise to report back regularly, and ask people to hold you to it. You might set consequences for yourself to make it even stronger.

These are some of the better motivators, in my experience, though you might be able to find others that work better for you, or some variations on the above.

The key is to think about these motivations regularly, and keep them at the front of your mind as you make decisions about your day and as you face resistance.

Procrastination

The moment of doing a task or habit arrives, and you feel resistance to actually doing that . . . and without thinking about it, you put it off. You avoid the discomfort of the task or habit, and try not to even think about it.

The solution is to be more mindful, and pause at the moment of resistance and urge to procrastinate. Don't just put it off, but face the resistance. This is a key habit to change, if you want to beat procrastination and be more disciplined.

At this moment, you should think about your deeper motivation. What will move you to push through the resistance and do what you know you want to do? Don't skip this step—think deeply about it, and be moved by it.

At the same time, you want to lower the resistance by making the habit or the task as small as possible. Just focus on getting started, and perhaps even tell yourself you just need to do a couple minutes of the task or habit. Take the smallest first step, and resistance isn't too great.

Finally, remove distractions and other options as much as you can, so you don't have anything that's easier than pushing through the resistance and doing this small, easy task.

Discipline

If you want to be more disciplined, it's a habit that you can strengthen. You have to truly want it, and find a deeper motivation for it. Commit yourself to developing the habit of discipline.

Then start small. Just pick one small thing to be disciplined about, and focus on that for at least a couple weeks, instead of trying to be disciplined with every single thing in your life at once. Like any muscle, the discipline muscle is best if you start easy and only gradually increase as your muscle gets stronger.

Pick something easy. Perhaps just do a 5-sentence journal every morning. Or put your clothes in the hamper for a month. Do 10 pushups every morning. Not all of these, just one!

As you work on this discipline muscle, follow the ideas above about motivation and beating procrastination, so you don't fall for those traps.

Finally, discipline has been proven to be lower when you're tired and stressed. So perhaps a good discipline area is getting more sleep, and then meditating or doing something else to lower your stress levels!

Chapter 36

Meditation and Mindfulness Habits

This is my favorite habit, and the one I think is most important—not only because it helps with all other habits, but because it can eventually lead to greater happiness and contentment in life.

However, for many people, sticking to a regularly meditation habit can be a struggle. And others want to remember to be more mindful throughout the day, which can be a challenge as well.

Let's talk briefly about each.

Daily Meditation Habit

What makes this habit difficult to stick with? First, most people don't actually enjoy the habit—it can be frustrating or boring, or fill you with uncertainty, if you feel like you're doing it wrong. Second, we're often in a rush to do the next thing we need to do (check email, take care of work tasks, respond to messages), and so sitting there doing nothing can make us feel anxious to get up and move on.

These are actually really good things to learn to deal with, because they're the same mental habits we have in all other activities, but we just don't often notice them. How can we deal with frustration, boredom, uncertainty, the need to rush and do the next task? By noticing the feelings but not automatically following the urges they result in. By returning to the moment and practicing with it.

Once we realize this, meditation can then be a place where we practice with accepting the moment and whatever arises. This is a practice that helps us in all areas of life, and when we realize this, then we can see meditation as a rewarding activity.

Lower the discomfort level by starting really small—even just two minutes of meditation the first week. Then five minutes for a couple weeks after that. Then 7 or 8 minutes. Then 10. Don't be in a rush to increase, just be patient and keep doing it daily.

Have a spot you meditate, and try to do it first thing in the morning, before you get caught in the rush of the day. Have a reminder that you'll definitely see when you first awake. Report to others each day after you do the habit. Don't let yourself skip it, just get your butt on the cushion and get started. Smile as you do so.

Forgetting to Be Mindful

If you have a meditation habit but want to carry the practice to the rest of your day, then you need to remember to be mindful. Some tips:

- Make at least one meal a mindful eating practice.
- Have your exercise be a mindful practice as well.

- Journal about being mindful all day, so you can review how you've done and look for ways to make improvements.

- Put reminders all around you—on your phone's lock screen, on your computer's wallpaper, physical reminders on your desk or near your bed.

- Use a computer reminder to remind you to be mindful of your surroundings every 20 or 25 minutes or so while you're online.

- Have certain cues remind you to check in and practice mindfulness: entering a room, getting in your car, looking at someone's face, putting on your clothes, getting in the shower, etc.

- Do all of these one at a time, practicing with that singular focus for at least a few days before adding another. Don't be in a rush to add more practices or cues.

Chapter 37

Sleep and Waking Early Habits

A common goal is to want to wake earlier, to get more done, feel less rushed in the morning, and enjoy a lovely quiet time of the day. And lots of people want to get to sleep earlier, which is obviously a linked habit.

When I started this blog, I had formed the habit of waking early, and enjoyed that for years. These days I don't get up super early most days (between 6:30–7AM lately) but I did learn a lot about forming this habit.

Going to sleep earlier is something I've struggled with for years, as I often have insomnia, but I do have some thoughts on this as well.

But my general and most important tip is this: **change your sleep habits gradually.** Most people who want to wake at 6AM (for example) will just try to set their alarm for 6AM and then struggle to get up. They also will struggle to get to sleep early enough. And that's because sleep patterns are hard to change. We have sleep rhythms that aren't easily shifted. So change gradually—just go to bed 10 minutes earlier and wake 10 minutes earlier at first, then after a few days, adjust another 10 minutes, and so on. Eventually you'll get to your new wake time, but you'll give yourself time to adjust.

Waking Earlier

Some tips:

- Again, wake earlier just a little at a time, starting with just 10 minutes earlier. Don't rush this.

- If you tend to hit the snooze button, put your alarm across the room. Use a regular alarm clock and your phone, in different places. Change your alarm tone regularly so you don't tune it out. Get loud or obnoxious tone if necessary, or use a wake-up service.

- Have something you're excited to do when you wake up. For example, if you're excited about meditation, yoga, sketching, having tea, writing a novel . . . plan to do that first thing.

- Jump out of bed with excitement when your alarm goes off!

- When you wake up, really focus on enjoying the beauty and quiet of the morning. It's lovely. Smile.

Getting To Sleep

We struggle to go to bed earlier, usually because we get stuck in online habits or watching TV or playing games—whatever we usually do late at night, it's hard to tear ourselves away. So the first habit is learning to pull away from your late night activity on time.

Some tips:

- Set an alarm or alert for a certain time to get away from your late-night activity and start getting ready for bed. Make this a hard-and-fast bedtime routine start time.

- When the alarm goes off, don't let yourself put it off. If you find yourself saying, "Just one more minute," pause. This is the resistance we talked about in Part I of this book—face it with mindfulness instead of just running from it.

- If you need it, ask a friend for help remembering or for help with accountability to sticking to this start time.

- Make your bedtime routine something relaxing and/or appealing—perhaps you take a bath or shower, or meditate with relaxing music, or tidy up and brush your teeth and journal, or pick a few things you're going to focus on in the morning and set things up so you're ready to go. Time this routine so you can start it on time to get to bed when you want to be in bed.

- Don't have any electronics or TV on in your sleeping area. This should be your space to be electronics-free. Make this another hard-and-fast rule or you won't get to sleep until late.

- Again, make your bedtime only gradually earlier—don't try to immediately go to bed two hours earlier than normal. It takes time to adjust going to sleep earlier.

- If it helps to read yourself to sleep, go ahead and do that. If it helps to listen to (relaxing) music, do that. If listening to informative but not exciting history podcasts helps you to sleep, do that. Figure out what works for you, but if it keeps you awake, drop that method.

- What often works for me is some kind of meditation— breath meditation or thinking about the beginning of my day in step-by-step detail, trying to remember and visualize every single thing I did when I woke up that day, in order. I often fall asleep within a few minutes of starting this visualization.

Chapter 38

Writing or Journaling Daily

For years, I had the idea that I would wake up early every morning and write . . . but for many years, I simply never did it regularly past the first day or two of inspiration. Then about 10 years ago, I formed the morning writing habit, and it has helped me to create my blog, courses and numerous books.

I've also always wanted to journal regularly, but it's always happened in starts and spurts, but I haven't been able to keep it going . . . until recently. Now I journal first thing in the morning, right after meditating. It's a great habit of reflection that helps me stick to all other habits and deepens my learning.

I don't recommend forming both these habits at once. Try one, get it going, and only once that's pretty solid should you try the other habit (though there's no need to do both). Let's look at some ideas for each.

Writing Daily

For me, writing is the most important work I do all day, so I prioritize it. I used to do it first thing every morning, but now that it's pretty solid, I put meditation, journaling, and setting my daily priorities before writing. I never skip the writing these days, unless I'm traveling.

Some ideas on getting it going:

- Have a really important motivation to get up and do it in the morning. Are you doing it to make the lives of others better in some way? To help yourself in a powerful way? Be clear on that reason, keep a note about it somewhere you won't forget it, and let it move you to action.

- If it's important to you, start the day with it. Perhaps get up, pee, drink some water, start the coffeemaker . . . then get started writing. Don't let yourself insert anything in between, like checking email, news or social media.

- Clear all distractions, turn off your network connection, shut off your phone, turn off all programs except your writing program. I recommend doing this the night before, so you're ready to start writing as soon as you turn on your computer.

- Some people really like writing longhand, with pen and paper. If you can do this, I recommend it, but I've been typing as a writer for 25 years, and am probably not ever going to change (even when writing input is done just by thinking).

- Have a writing spot, maybe a writing playlist to block out all distractions, maybe tea or coffee to make the experience more pleasant.

- Start small, with just 5 minutes of writing. Do it in bursts, getting up to stretch, breathe, have a glass of water. Pat yourself on the back. Then try another burst. You can just start with one 5-minute burst for the first week, then two the second. Eventually lengthen your bursts to 10 minutes, 12, then 15.

- When resistance comes up (and it will), don't run from it. Face it. Allow yourself to do nothing but sit there, or write.

Journaling

Journaling can be done in many ways, but I simply like to dump whatever's on my mind into the journal. And I reflect on what I did yesterday, what I've been learning, some things I want to do in the near or far future. Sometimes I think about life aspirations. But there are lots of options.

Some ideas for forming the habit:

- Try a 5-sentence journal. It's quick and easy, and it gets you into the habit.

- I also love a gratitude journal—what are you grateful for right now? I find it a great way to appreciate what I have in my life, rather than focusing on what I don't have.

- Do the habit as early in the day as you can, if you want to form the habit and be consistent about it. However, if you have no doubts about whether you'll actually do it, an end-of-day reflective journal is often very helpful.

- I use the journaling app DayOne, though it's just for the Mac. You can add photos, have it backed up online, use it on multiple devices, and it's pretty simple to use.

- If you're not consistent about it, ask a friend for some help sticking to it. I use my Habit Zen habit app to check off when I meditated and journaled, and I find it rewarding to check off each day after I've done it.

Chapter 39

Financial Habits

I'm going to admit that I'm not a financial wizard, but I did spend a few years getting out of a lot of debt, and I did save a good amount of money and then learned to invest it automatically. I did all of that by forming some small financial habits that I definitely didn't have before.

I'm not going to be able to do personal finances any justice in this short chapter, but I'll briefly share some thoughts on developing good financial habits:

- My worst financial habit in the past was not facing them. I knew my finances were a mess, so I'd avoid thinking about debts and bills and budgeting. I shoved past-due bill notices in a drawer, racked up debt without knowing how much, and generally put off dealing with the whole mess as long as I could, until it came crashing down. So your first financial habit is learning to face them, even if they're scary. You can do that by just doing a little at a time.

- A good start is just listing your debts and bills. Make a list of them all, taking 5–10 minutes a day until your list is done. Then spend those 5–10 minutes each day listing their due dates, monthly payment amounts and overall debt. This might require finding paper bills or looking online for this info. Start creating a "financial health sheet."

- Another good way to spend your daily financial time is to start adding up your monthly expenses—how much do you spend on groceries, eating out, entertainment and books, shopping and clothes, household bills, transportation, housing, education, etc? You can have a program like Mint.com try and add everything up for you, or put it in a spreadsheet.

- Then start looking at how much you spend each month vs. how much you're earning. Are you outspending your earnings, and by how much? Are you making more than you spend, and what are you doing with the difference?

- If you have savings and investment, congratulations! Put those numbers on your financial health sheet too. Try automating savings, and then investments.

- If you're in debt, try creating a plan for paying this off. See how much you can scrounge each month by cutting expenses—this will be your debt repayment amount. Cut cut cut until this amount is as high as you can get it. Now plan which debt to pay off first—either the one with the highest interest (recommended) or the one with the smallest overall debt total (so you can have the satisfaction of paying it off). Which debt will be paid off after that? You can actually plan how many months it will take to pay off each debt if you know your "debt repayment" amount (or "debt snowball" amount in Dave Ramsey terms).

- When one debt is paid off, take the amount you were paying and pay it to the next debt. And so on—it should get bigger and bigger as more of your debts are paid off. Again, see Dave Ramsey for more on the debt snowball method.

- Housing and transportation are the biggest expenses for most people—focusing on lowering these amounts can make more difference than focusing on, say, groceries or entertainment. Find a smaller place, use a cheaper car (or use a bike if you can), and you can pay off debts faster and then save and invest faster.

- Once you've done all this, you don't need to spend time every day on finances. I like to spend a little time every week making sure all the bills are paid and my accounts are up-to-date (again, I used Mint.com to automatically update all this info), then a little time each month looking at my overall financial picture and making adjustments as needed.

- Automate as much as you can. If you have a debt re-payment plan, automate the debt payments. Automate bill payments. Automate savings and investments. The more you can automate, the less you think about it, and the better it all works.

- You should immediately try to spend less than you earn, cutting expenses until that's true. The bigger the difference, the better. Use the difference to pay debt, save an emergency fund, and then invest. Try to save/invest 10% of your income, increasing it to 20% if possible. My friend J. D. Roth (of MoneyBoss.com) recommends a 50% savings rate! He says to cut down housing and transportation expenses, and increase income however you can.

- Investing is simple: get a Vanguard account and invest in low-fee index funds (like the Vanguard 500 that indexes the SandP 500). Most fund managers don't beat the rate of these index funds after you take away their fees, and non-professional investors like us certainly aren't going to beat their rates.

In the end, it just takes finding the courage to take small steps regularly to get a clear picture of your finances, to start moving in the right direction, and to automate things so that you get in better and better shape.

Chapter 40

Notes on Other Habits

I can't do a chapter on every type of habit, so I thought I'd share a few brief thoughts on habits that people want to form in this chapter.

- **Arriving on time**: If you're constantly late, the real habit is to leave on time. Which means getting ready to leave on time. Which means pulling yourself away from your computer or TV at the right time to start getting ready. See the chapter on getting to sleep for tips on this, as it's essentially the same habit as starting to get ready for bed on time. It's good to figure out how long it takes you to get places, rather than underestimating travel time, and also figure out how long it takes you to get ready—so time both of these for awhile until you know. Put in extra time for traffic and other unexpected delays—it's better to show up early and read while you wait.

- **Morning routine**: I suggest starting with as small a morning routine as possible, getting that solidified, and then only slowly adding one habit a month. But don't add too many. For example, if you start waking a little earlier, meditate and journal. As you get up a little earlier than that, you might add reading or writing (but not both at once). Stop after 4–5 habits because otherwise it becomes a house of cards ready to come tumbling down.

- **Focusing**: The key to focus is clearing distractions, and not letting yourself switch tasks. Pick an important task to work on, and tell yourself, "For the next X minutes, I'm going to do nothing but this task." Pull yourself away from everything else, and clear everything but the one tool you need to do this task. Shut off the Internet. Notice when you want to put off the task or switch to something else, and instead just sit there and face the resistance with mindfulness.

- **Calendar and to-do lists**: For me, there are two key calendar habits—remembering to put items on the calendar when I make an appointment or hear about something I want to remember on specific date, and checking my calendar every morning. For my to-do list, it's basically the same two habits except I put items that aren't on a specific day/time—I have to remember to put items on the list, and remember to check the list in the morning. My habit is to look at my calendar and to-do list in the morning, after journaling, and set my agenda and priorities. Remembering to put things on the list and calendar takes more time, but you can do it if you give the habit focus for a couple weeks (have a note reminding you at your desk). I use a "Today" list, a "Later" list for things I'm going to do soon but not today, and a "Someday" list for ideas for future projects.

- **Doing less, taking on fewer projects**: If you're overwhelmed, the key is to learn to say No. When you have the choice to take on a project, it's helpful to look at your list of projects and decide what needs to take priority. Start trying to get a better idea of how long projects take, how long meetings or calls take, how long a trip takes of your time (trip planning, communication, and decompressing, for example), and so on. This way you know what you're saying Yes to, if given the option, instead of underestimating the commitment. In general, it's better to have fewer commitments than too many, in my experience.

- **Decluttering**: This can be a small daily habit where you spend just 10 minutes decluttering one area. Pick a spot (say your kitchen counter) and clear away as many items as you can for donation, recycling, or giving to friends. Put them in a box and take action later, making a weekly trip to donation/recycling. After a few days, you'll probably have decluttered one area, move on to the next, then the next. Soon you'll be living in a minimalist Zen temple!

- **Taking time to decompress**: Sometimes we just rush through our entire days, and have no time for relaxing. Eva and I have developed a habit of having a glass of wine and watching our favorite TV show after dinner. I work hard, spend time with the kids, workout, work some more, until dinner comes, then it's decompress and get offline after that. Other ideas for decompress time include having tea, taking a bath, going for a walk, spending some quiet time reading, doing yoga, meditating, taking a short nap in the afternoon. I think it's important to find a time for it and say, "No online stuff at this time."

- **Prioritizing health and self care**: This isn't really a habit, but the way you can prioritize it is to first say that this is really important to you and needs to become a priority. And then to pick one health or self-care habit to start with, and give it your full effort. Just one health/self-care habit at a time, and start small with it. Good places to start are meditation, gradually eating healthier, doing a little exercise, brushing your teeth and flossing.

- **Brushing teeth and flossing**: Have a time when you brush your teeth and floss in the morning, and then put in your full effort to do it every day until it becomes automatic. Have reminders, both digital and physical. And enjoy those activities mindfully and with gratitude, rather than rushing to get to the next thing. Make flossing as easy as you can, even just starting with flossing one tooth.

- **Daily yoga**: Honestly, I've never formed this habit, though it's something I'd like to do. But I think it's a habit like meditation or exercise, where you just need to set aside time early in your day (or at the end), commit to it, have reminders and accountability, and face the resistance with mindfulness when it gets in your way.

- **Dealing with difficult emotions**: The best way to learn to deal with difficult emotions—which isn't easy—is to form the habit of meditation. In meditation, we eventually learn not to attach too much to the thought patterns that come up, including the ones that cause difficult emotions. We learn to notice when the emotion is coming up, and with practice, we can learn to face the physical feeling that's in our bodies and stay with it, just facing it with friendliness. This is an important practice, and I highly recommend it.

- **Developing confidence**: We develop confidence when we deal with our insecurities about ourselves, when we develop trust that we're good enough and that we'll be OK. Again, I think meditation is the best way to deal with this. If you meditate, start to notice your basic goodness that underlies all your thoughts, emotions, and experiences. And see that you're OK, in every moment.

- **Reducing the phone habit**: Put a reminder on your phone's lock screen: "Be in the moment." Pause when you see this reminder before doing anything on your phone. See your urge to check things on the phone with mindfulness. Stay with the urge but don't act on it. Put the phone down and spend a few seconds just noticing this moment around you. Smile. Repeat as often as you need, only using the phone when you need to actually do something important.

- **Stop drinking diet soda or alcohol, quitting smoking, reducing shopping**: See the chapter on Quitting a Bad Habit for help with these.

Thank You For Reading

I'm deeply grateful to you for reading this book. I hope you found it helpful, and I wish you the best in your habit creation experiments.

About the Author

Leo Babauta is the creator of Zen Habits, and author of the *Zen Habits* book as well as *Essential Zen Habits*. He has helped thousands of people change their habits, simplify their lives and practice mindfulness through his blog and his Sea Change membership program. He lives in Davis, California with his wife and six kids (several of whom are now adults!). He's a vegan, and enjoys running, reading, meditating, lifting weights and hiking.

Printed in the USA
CPSIA information can be obtained
at www.ICGtesting.com
LVHW080938100124
768241LV00084B/3631